MW00882515

# Jesus Religion

6-2009

Laura,

I've enjoyed the
journey into the
world of ghosts &
spirits with you!

I trust this book
speaks to you...

Many Blessings!
Chuck
"Yours Charles"

A CRITICAL EXAMINATION OF CHRISTIAN INSANITY

# Jesus Religion

## Louis Charles

A GUIDE TO UNDERSTANDING THE TRUE
MESSAGE OF YESHUA

Published by Angels & Ghosts, LLC
c/o www.JesusReligion.com and Louis Charles
truthwithinyou@yahoo.com

Cover design and artwork by Louis Charles
Copyright © 2009 www.JesusReligion.com and Angels & Ghosts, LLC

Published in the United States of America

ISBN: 1442157240
EAN-13: 9781442157248
Non-Fiction: Religion: Spirituality

Dedicated to my loving wife, Becky

Without your support I could never
have embarked on this journey...

Thank you to Walt, Marty and countless others
who helped me find the path to freedom...

# Table of Contents

# Forward

After 12 years of seeking to further understand higher truth, in order to gain my freedom from harmful Christian teachings, I knew it was time to write this book. Having formerly succumbed to Fundamentalist Christian ideas concerning Hell and eternal punishment, I had always worried about my salvation and the inevitable future torment of "unsaved" family and friends. It was very difficult to shed such fears, because I was also taught that the Bible was God's perfect word. If something was in the Bible, God had said it, and it was therefore impossible to discount. For years, my mind was trapped into believing the worst imaginable fate for mankind was possible. After finding the path that changed my life, the falseness of religion eventually became clearer over time. I know there are others out in the world like me, who know something is wrong with Christianity's claims. Some may still be sitting in the back of a church service somewhere on Sundays, while others have possibly left Christianity altogether. Wherever you are in your spiritual journey, this book is for you. Use it as your guide to help distinguish the true path from the false. My goal is simply to free more people.

The structure of this book is quite loose but is intently focused on attacking traditional Christianity (especially Fundamentalist and Evangelical ideas) and its core philosophies. Though I take a risk by doing so, I feel I can no longer bury my head to what I see so clearly.  Consequently, some of my stories and thoughts may, at times, seem repetitious.  But, the falsehoods I attempt to dispel can be difficult for people to initially comprehend.  There truly is a method behind what may seem to be my madness.  The writing draws from personal experience, historical events, as well as biblical references in order to convey ideas.  The words of this book can be used to touch different people in different ways, no matter where they are in their spiritual travels.  Though some may become angered at what I write, this is a natural response to differences in opinion.  For some, it may take time to consider and learn new ideas.  Be patient with me, as well as yourself, remaining open to what is shared between these covers.  If you are unable to accept what you read, put the book away for awhile.  A day may come to re-open it and consider the insights once again.  Everyone has their own unique time for learning what is needed.  Life has a way of directing us toward the things we require in order to eventually arrive at the same destination - truth.  Some will absorb what they read within these pages like dry bread sopping up warm, healthy soup.  Others may have ears that are plugged, being unable to spiritually discern one truth found within the pages.  Be patient.

The thoughts I attempt to share came to me over a period of time in my life that compassed some 30 years in total.  I might say that writing a book about my journey has been like putting a period at the end of a very long sentence.  Looking back, I am truly thankful for what I have learned through the total experience. Yet, what you are about to read is really only a small portion of what I came to know through the teaching of Spirit. I was not alone in hearing many of the messages I share but had countless others who joined me on my journey. Over the years, they have provided excellent confirmation to me during the times I needed it most. It is amazing how others, who can be of assistance to us, will surface in our lives when we least expect it. Allow new people to invade your life, for we become teachers of each other, like iron sharpening iron.

There is much more to share beyond this book that perhaps I will publish in the future. The notes I began recording in the late 1990's eventually became the foundation for the following pages, some of which first appeared on-line in late 2002. My website, www.JesusReligion.com, became a small depository of short writings used to reach others who were looking for peace and freedom from faulty Christian teachings. Christians, who were seeking relief from religious fears, would occasionally search for help through use of the Internet. It was my goal to attempt to present some of my thoughts to such seekers in order to assist them in thinking differently. As you can imagine, my e-mail inbox often received letters of thanks from strangers whom the articles helped, as well as scorn from those who elected to defend the traditional Christian faith. No matter, for I have continued to write what I hear deep within me, being compelled to write this book as a continuation of the website articles. I am of the opinion, the more who read and hear, the better. People need to be freed from their own self-destructive ways of thinking, myself included. So it is, there are two paths from which we all may choose.

One never knows where life's road may lead. When I choose to follow Spirit, my higher self, often I am able to find great enjoyment through various adventures. For example, while writing these chapters, my inner guide had urged me to make contact with other people beyond my typical sphere of relationships. Some of them are former colleagues, friends, or distant family whom I felt compelled to spend time with. By doing so, I learn from them; allowing past mistakes in my thinking to be healed through seeing humanity with a new pair of eyes. This experiment in relationships has also brought me to new friendships, while also understanding it may be time for some older companions to fade to the background for a season. I find life exhilarating when I take time to allow myself to observe and contemplate the lessons that can always be found around us. Acting like a mirror, the world outside of us can truly reflect back the things we need to see. Lessons can be learned from everything we experience, so why not seek to understand that which we may require? I encourage you to embark on your own personal spiritual journey; for it is the only way you will know true inner peace. It is the good and right path. There is nothing more exciting than receiving a revelation of truth, something that is indeed life-changing and personally relevant. When we know the truth within us, peace, freedom and joy are its fruits. Know that there is so much more to life beyond what most of us have been taught, or we could ever imagine. And, if you learn anything from the following pages, let it be the decision to follow the ever-wise guide of your heart.

# 1 In The Beginning

This story begins when I was maybe 13 years old. Our neighbors would invite me to go to church with them occasionally. One Sunday morning, I elected to go with them to their "Bible Church." I remember the long ride out in the country as we neared the small Bible believer's assembly on the outside of town. Eventually, we arrived, attended Sunday school and then the main church service. After struggling to listen to a rather boring sermon about the only authorized and authentic translation of the Bible, the 1611 King James Version, I was later asked by the preacher to go with him alone into a side room. Catching me completely off-guard, I reluctantly agreed to follow the man, and so the door was closed behind us. The preacher turned to me and demanded I get on my knees, for I was a sinner. He told me to repeat after him, as he was going to lead me in prayer to accept Jesus as my savior, so I would have eternal life. Being young, naive and frightened, I repeated the eloquent prayer he recited before me. My words seemed hollow to me, but I would do just about anything to get out of that room; therefore, I decided immediately to get this experience over and behind me, or so it seemed. Afterward, the preacher joyfully told me I was now "saved." I soon headed home from the small church with my neighbors, but little did I know then that what had just happened to me would affect me for the rest of my life.

Some people would think that my "accepting Jesus" was a good thing. But for me, it was the beginning of my personal hell. The frightening seeds the preacher had put within my mind caused me to fear eternal punishment. I had to know the truth about this salvation of which he spoke, for I had never before heard of or even considered that I could be punished in a fiery place of torment after I die one day. You see, a man put his fear into my thinking, and I chose to accept that what he had told me was true. I didn't believe him at first, but his fear grew within me over the next several years, eventually paralyzing me by the time I was 19 years old. By age 21, I had been thoroughly confused by a co-worker who told me that what we did on Earth surely sent us to Hell. I told him that I was already saved and repeated for him my story of accepting Jesus at the small Bible church, several years prior. But, my co-worker had been converted to a legalistic Christian denomination while spending time in prison for murder, and so my supposed conversion to Christ was not real in his eyes. And so, his doubts soon became my doubts, as well. He believed that every little thing we did could send a person to Hell forever. If a woman didn't wear a dress and have long hair, she was going to Hell. If a person smoked, imbibed a little alcohol, or swore occasionally, that person also was going to Hell. Quite frankly, his beliefs spooked me worse than before, as my mind often recollected the preacher forcing me to my knees and praying the "Sinner's Prayer." Over time, this man's fears brought to surface my inner turmoil, causing my mind to enter into a frenzied panic. I remember rushing home after work one day and telling my wife we were both going to Hell, and we needed to do something about it. Feeling the need to be rescued, we did what most people do who are looking for answers about God: we went to church. I can remember talking to various pastors I would come in contact with about salvation and Hell. I was soon frustrated to find that so many of them disagreed with one another concerning the finality of salvation. Was it once saved, always saved, or could a person actually lose their salvation after accepting Jesus Christ? Thoughts such as these bugged me to no end. The Baptists believed that once a person accepts Jesus as their Lord and Savior, that person can never go to Hell. But other denominational ministers told me that one's salvation certainly could be lost, and cited opposing Bible verses, such as *"Work out your salvation with fear and trembling."* They did so in order to attempt to prove their theological position regarding salvation was the more sound approach, when compared with the Baptists. "How could men of God not agree on the truth collectively about such an important work?" I wondered. Feeling determined to know the truth, I found myself studying the Bible daily, jumping head first into Christianity and its theological teachings.

The church we chose was one my wife had attended for much of her childhood. The head minister paid us a visit and seemed nice enough, so we began attending Bible studies there. Eventually, after many conversations with the ministers about my fears concerning salvation, I was baptized by immersion in water. My baptism occurred in December of 1986. From that time on, every night I would study the Bible for hours. I devoured as much Christian teaching as possible through reading books, attending Bible study classes, and listening to Evangelical radio programs. I would work hard on studying chapters of the Bible, making notes concerning interpretations of

passages, and seeking to understand the words of
the original Bible languages. At that time in my life,
I felt I could find answers to all life's questions
through the various subjects contained within
the *Good Book*. I did not waiver in my studies, for I
was thoroughly convinced the Bible was "God's
Word," and that it was without error and a letter
from God to all of humanity. My hunger for truth
led me straight into Fundamentalist Christian ideas.

As the years progressed, church leaders took notice
of my biblical knowledge, and I soon enjoyed
leading a youth group of teens at church. This
eventually led to my teaching a young adult Sunday
school class. Before I knew it, I was a deacon of the
church, serving communion to shut-ins and visiting
people in nursing homes. A few more years passed,
and I found myself giving some instruction to a few
of the church elders concerning a difficult situation
involving the pastor. Afterward, I was then asked
to become an elder of the congregation, in the hopes
I could assist them with church matters. Through
all these experiences, I never sought to be a leader,
for I had only one desire: I wanted to know the truth
about God and my relationship with him. The
salvation question still bothered me; but though I
felt I was working hard to become a super-

Christian, I had no idea why the nagging within me persisted.

In 1995, I was completely taken by surprise. Being very involved in a church similar to the Baptist denomination, I was unaware of the presence of Spirit. Even now, I find it hard to believe I never knew that a tangible, spiritual presence could be perceived, or even felt. You see, I was of the mind that God is Spirit, and that simply meant God was invisible. One day, what I would describe as being a weighty presence came upon me, and I was changed. Instantly, I was aware of Spirit. I had never before experienced an invisible, loving, peaceful, and joyful presence, that I could physically feel embrace me. This tangible presence stayed with me for about a week. The only way I can now describe this experience was that I felt new, maybe re-born, and cleansed within. Little did I know it at the time, but I was soon to discover that other Christian denominations, such as Pentecostals and Charismatics, teach about such an experience which they term the "baptism of the spirit." They teach that everyone can receive this life-changing, in-filling of the Holy Spirit. So after my so-called awakening, I decided, of course, to study the Holy Spirit and the accompanying charismatic phenomena. Not too long after my new acquaintance with Spirit, I perceived a directive inside me: "Lay hands on people." Not quite understanding why I should hear and do such a thing, I decided to put myself in a position to be able to test out this idea. Being a church leader, it was quite simple for me to suggest that after church services the elders should ask if anyone is sick, and invite the afflicted to the front whereby we could place our hands upon them and pray. And so, I found a way to begin laying my hands on top of people's heads, as we anointed them with oil and prayed for them. Shockingly, people I prayed for were touched by the Spirit, and had similar spiritual experiences, even healings, among other Pentecostal manifestations which are not necessary to mention. Soon, an exciting spiritual wave of what I shall coin "charismania" swept through our dry, little congregation; and I found myself teaching, occasionally preaching, and of course still praying for whomever I could get my hands upon. It was a wonderful and exciting time. Not only I, but others were now experiencing this tangible, spirit presence, and we wanted more of it. Eventually, the pastor, then most all of the elders had their own personal experiences with Spirit. I can still recall some of us driving eighteen hours to Pensacola,

Florida to participate in a worship service at the
Brownsville Assembly of God revival!
Unfortunately, the change which we experienced
together as elders would eventually divide the
church; for some members wished to remain
stagnant and safe, while others desired to be
touched by the Spirit and transformed. It was
impossible to please everyone, and this spiritual
awakening became quite controversial. But through
it all, I still wanted only one thing: the truth.

During that time in my life, I felt closer to God than
I had ever been, so I was riding pretty high for
awhile. However, the more I sought direction
inwardly through the leading of Spirit, the more I
began perceiving the answers I had been seeking for
a long time. One day a man visited our church, who
would soon confirm what I knew deep within me.
He came as a mentor to assist the church
leadership. By this time in 1996, I was now
Chairman of the Elders and looking for advice on
how we could best steer the congregation towards
God's will. Simply put, I felt that if we could line up
with what God wanted us to do, then the church
would be blessed with members, finances, and
ministries. The man visiting with us was adept at
helping church leaders discover God's will for local

assemblies. In other words, he would help Christian leaders discover what the church mission should be in making a difference within the community. However, after sitting through this meeting with him and the elders for awhile, I had only one question that nagged at me: "Could it be God's will to shut the doors?" The man replied, "Yes, it could very well be God's will to shut the doors of this church." Understand that during my tenure of a decade at the same church, I had observed several congregational splits occur for a variety of reasons. It seemed that whenever things were going well, something would rear its ugly head and divide the people, as if this church congregation were not meant to exist any longer. As a leader, I became tired of working to try and keep things together. Nothing seemed to work, and our efforts seemed futile to me. I truly felt like I was fighting against God, not for him. So, I was very surprised that what I had known deep down (but previously kept hidden inside me), came bursting forth as a question regarding could it be God's desire to shut the church doors. I knew from that moment on, that I could no longer suppress what I was hearing within my deepest being. Just because a majority of people think it best to begin and maintain a religious organization, doesn't mean that they have God ordaining and supporting their efforts. It was only a few months later that I handed my adult Bible study class over to another, because I knew I was to do so. And soon after that, I just knew it was time for me and my family to leave.

No one understood my reasons for leaving the church at the time, and today many within the congregation still think of me as being a heretic for doing so. My wife, three children, and I had our lives intertwined within our former church family. Leaving them behind was most difficult, a decision which all of us struggled to come to terms with. Most all of our friends were developed through the church we had participated in for eleven years. Our grandparents attended there, as well. Part of me never wanted to leave, but knew I had to. The elders, and congregation included, did not understand our departure, but a few weeks after coming to this difficult decision, we made it a point to speak to everyone before leaving in June 1997. It truly was a sad day for us, but for a couple months, some of our church friends would call or visit trying to convince us to return to the congregation. Other friends of ours also felt they were to leave the small church. When it became clear that we were not coming back, being further fueled by the loss of a

few more members, the church leadership began to
tell the congregation that we were lost. When the
pastor and elders heard we had visited another
church within the same county, they elected to
inform that church's pastor that we were misguided
and trouble. Their senseless persecution and
personal attacks against us took my wife and me
years to put behind us. Despite the struggles and
lost relationships, we learned a lot. My wife and I
eventually became free from fear, free from religion,
and free from false relationships that existed only
under certain pretenses. Neither of us ever could or
would go back again. To do so now, would be as
awful as a dog returning to consume its own vomit.
As the number of days grew since the day we left,
the more we became able to fully comprehend the
religion that had unwittingly enslaved us. Twenty
years had passed since my initial indoctrination into
Christianity, and it took me walking away from the
Jesus religion to be able to comprehend how
horribly it had choked the life right out of me.

Leaving the religion, supposedly founded upon the
teachings of Jesus, finally permitted me to grasp
what the sayings of this man might really have
meant. All of the false beliefs I had accumulated
over two decades, eventually dissipated one by one,

as I found myself still being drawn to Bible passages. The same inner knowing which I shall call Spirit, helped to enlighten the scriptures to me in a new way. Because the Bible was formerly used as a weapon to *bind me* to a literal, Fundamentalist Christian theology, the same biblical passages were necessary to be used as a tool to help *unbind me* from such fearful teachings. By facing the fear and its source, I found it no longer had any control over me. Within me, I found great peace and comfort in having the same scriptures revealed to me as having a higher spiritual meaning than what I had formerly been taught. My teacher through all this was (who I could only assume as being) Spirit who first made its presence known to me a few years prior. The excitement I felt during these times as my eyes were opened was incredible. I couldn't get enough, and the more I understood, the more I was driven to know even more. Each grain of knowledge I absorbed was like having another chain removed from my mind. You may think it difficult to go on a spiritual journey all alone. But know that no one is ever truly alone. During my time of gaining my freedom, others who were also hearing these same truths within themselves were brought to me as confirmation, often becoming at times my spiritual mentors. These peers became close friends of mine,

as we seemed cast together on an adventure in
pursuit of truth.  It was simply wonderful to share
with each other what we were individually hearing
within our deepest parts.  At the time I kept
thinking, "Could this really be happening to me?"
For over ten years, I searched to find the truth.  Now
my world had been turned upside down, and I
finally felt for the first time everything was
becoming new.  By 1999, I had jotted down quite a
bit of what I had been spiritually hearing, but was
not sure for what purpose.  Since that time, I have
continued listening and writing about what has
been revealed to me from within.

Perhaps now is the time to share some of these
teachings with those who are also seeking the way
to their own spiritual freedom.  For me, I couldn't
hear what was deep within me until I was willing to
lay down all I thought I knew, which was really
only what I had been taught by others.  Regrettably,
I had grabbed hold of traditional Christian
teachings, studied them, taught them, thus believing
them as being the only way to God.  No one told me
I hadn't gone deep enough.  Scrambling to a local
church will not bring the true inner freedom one
desires.  For that matter, joining any religion and
believing you'll find answers from someone else,

will never lead one down the inner path to truth. Your "salvation" has nothing to do with believing in Jesus, going to church, reading the Bible, saying prayers, taking communion or even being baptized. Are you willing to lay down all the traditions of men and religious ideas that you learned from others? In subsequent chapters, I will challenge you to do so. Are you ready for what lies ahead? If so, you may find the following pages quite challenging to your beliefs.

Being a former Bible teacher, I sought to understand and follow the teachings of Jesus. Over years of study, one thing began to emerge as being clear: a religion had been created in Jesus' name by men who were either in religious leadership, political power, or both. In fact, the more I studied the basic Fundamentalist Christian doctrines, the more they did not make sense. They seemed to me as being created to gain control over others. Traditional Christian doctrines, frankly, are not freeing people, nor are they bringing peace, joy and love to mankind. They are sadly enslaving many into bondage through fear and falsehoods.

So why write this book? I wanted to share what I have found to be truth, so maybe I could help those who are struggling within Christian congregations. It does not matter what Christian denomination or organization one might be affiliated with, as the body of Christ is people; and the truths of Jesus' real message is timeless and in great need to be heard by all today. By initially sharing my story, it should become apparent that I understand what it is to be a Christian believer. This gives me an advantage, because not only do I understand Fundamentalist Christian doctrines, I now also see them for what they are: fearful teachings designed to apprehend and maintain converts. Fully comprehending both perspectives has allowed me to not only be empathetic toward the Christian condition but has also driven me to know what is needed to become free from such injurious a religion. In short, I have been there, done that, got the t-shirt. But having this knowledge can be helpful to you, the seeker of truth. For I understand what you, as a Christian, believe. I know where your fears lie. Therefore, I will speak to your condition in subsequent chapters, ever working to free your mind from the fallacies that perhaps subsist.

I should further clarify my mission, by stating emphatically that it is not my intention to attack Christians. But, my examination of the Christian theology does indeed attack Christian leaders and teachers who continue to instruct and support false religion that was created in Jesus' name. At times, I may find common ground with both the religious and the atheist, but I shall never leave such people unchallenged, or support those who seek to influence others through fearful ideas of a vengeful god. I feel that the man we have named Jesus (his real name was more likely *Yeshua*), did indeed have something important to share with this world. My opinion concerning this has been formed from what I have been able to deduce as being the teachings that still must have evolved from Yeshua. And so, it seems clear to me that his higher ideals shared within parables are the most important examples of spiritual truth from which we can seek to understand. I, therefore, find it necessary to use some Bible passages within this book. I do so, for there are those who need scripture verses to help them understand the message they personally need to hear. By allowing me this liberty, I hope to enlighten the reader with spirituality, and not religion. Jesus never founded a religion; but men who came after Yeshua indeed created Christianity. Religion is not truth, but simply theories, ideas, legends, and fables ever hopelessly pointing people outwardly for life's answers, being initially created and perpetually sustained from fear within the human mind.

This book then serves as confirmation to those who know deep down that there is something fundamentally wrong with traditional Christianity. The traditional doctrines seem at first truthful, but when examined, they fall very short of being divinely-inspired. I struggle when I listen to preachers in churches across America recite such nonsense, some being no better than well-paid pulpit puppets, reciting erroneous doctrines they learned from others. They use the Bible as an authoritative tool, in order to cause others to fearfully believe that what they promote is indeed the truth. Their message ever wreaks of condemnation, guilt, doubt, and every other form of fear imagined; a method used quite effectively to seduce and hold onto believers of the Christian faith. Such ministers of "God" are quick to latch onto vulnerable people who seek answers, by claiming that all of mankind is inherently evil, undeserving, helpless, powerless, damnable, and lost. Yet, in spewing such rubbish from under the guise of an adorned church building, elegant clothing, and seemingly authoritative title and church position, they unknowingly create emotional trauma for countless millions.  Surprisingly, church leaders may even mean well, mistakenly thinking that by doing such a "good work" they are saving people from eternal torment.  Sadly, though, they are unable to comprehend the damage they produce, harming the very people they were intending to rescue.

Yet, what is missed by those who claim to teach and preach Jesus, is the fact that he never condemned people who were truly seeking answers.  He spoke of looking at things differently, while attacking religious leaders of his day who were harming the common people in much the same way as today's Christian leaders.  Yeshua related much of his message through parables that were not to be understood literally, as today's theologians would have us believe.  By using parables, Yeshua marveled crowds with spiritual wisdom - truth.  He only asked that each person listen within their deeper self for the answers hidden within his parables, as he warned there is a broad way that leads to destruction; but a narrow way that few find that leads to life.  That narrow way is what I wish to express further in this book.  It is ultimately a way to hear the message of Jesus differently than you might have ever heard it taught within a church.

# 2  The Word of God?

After I became aware of Spirit and saw the results of laying hands and praying for others, my desire for greater spiritual wisdom grew even more intense.  It was at this time that I began meditating, so I could silence the mundane thoughts in my head in order to be able to better hear the deeper knowledge of my heart more clearly.  The messages I heard were not from an audible voice but were simply a "knowing" found deep within me.  Often, this *knowing* of higher truth would cause me to contemplate such thoughts more deeply.  Over time I was able to discern answers to my greatest questions concerning life and my place in it.  This still, small voice of Spirit was soon revealed to me as being the true word of God.  What better way could there be to acquire perfect life-direction, than to go directly to the very source of life itself, which is Spirit?  I knew I had found the real voice, the true word of the Divine.  Yet, this is in stark contrast to what many Christians believe to be God's word.  Today, Fundamentalist and Evangelical Christian teachings both claim that the Bible is the *Word of God*.  This idea of the Bible being perfect is not ancient, for it has grown in popularity only within the past century.

So, in examining Christian theology, I find it necessary to first address a common belief within Christianity that the Bible is God's word, infallible, inerrant and divinely-inspired.  When such claims are made by supposed theologians, it is done so in order to establish within the minds of the fearful that there is no argument that can be made against what is printed between the book's covers.  Christian teachers prefer their students believe that God breathed divine thoughts into the minds of men, who then faithfully recorded them onto manuscripts, effectively creating a godly book of law that is to be reverenced and seldom challenged.  But, the fact is, the Bible is full of contradictions, even containing plagiarism, not to mention incorrect language translations.  It would be safer to believe that an almighty god would fare much better by speaking to each individual personally, than to trust in letters that have been copied, altered, and mistranslated by hundreds, if not thousands of individuals over time.

Many Christians are taught, and so believe, that the Bible contains original books which were put together by men as God inspired them to compose such writings; that this same collection of documents is perfect in sharing God's true nature and desire for mankind.  In short, it is taught that this assembly of texts is God-ordained, holy, and never to be questioned.  Nothing further could be from the truth. The construction of the Bible we know today is somewhat interesting, yet, questionable and quite complicated to understand.  The books contained within its covers can be summed up as being the *Hebrew Bible* (also known as the *Old Testament*), with the *New Testament* being comprised of what are known as the four *Gospels*, *The Acts of the Apostles*, the

*Epistles*, and *The Revelation of John*. This collective group of writings can vary, depending upon the Christian denomination. Some denominations have additional texts included within their biblical canon. Most notably, the Catholic Bible contains the Apocrypha, in addition to the sixty-six books found within the typical Christian Bible. What is important to understand is the letters collected and bound into book form, namely the Bible, only comprise a small portion of what was being read within early Christian communities.

Let's look briefly at the Bible and the early church. Christians in the first few centuries would meet together and listen to the reading of various texts. Because ninety percent of the ancient population were illiterate, Christian writings were read aloud publicly, allowing listeners to hear the various messages and stories. The documents, later collected to form the New Testament, were only a small portion of what was being read within the gatherings of early Christians. For example, there were other Gospels, additional Acts, numerous Epistles, Apocalypses, accounts of martyrdom and persecutions, letters attacking heresies, communications of Christian instruction, teaching, and defenses for the faith. The twenty-seven books that eventually became the Bible's New Testament were argued about for hundreds of years. This assembly of writings was sometimes suggested for reading within Christian gatherings, yet their inclusion was not always agreed upon due to challenges of authenticity. I think it is good for Christians to be aware that there were many letters written in order to recount stories of Yeshua and his followers, explain and even defend beliefs concerning them, encourage others in the faith, and to foretell possible future events yet to come. The following writings are some examples of manuscripts that were not included in the Bible: The Letter of Clement, The Didache, Book of Enoch, Book of Jasher, Gospel of Thomas, Gospel of Judas, Gospel of Mary, The Apocalypse of Peter, Epistle of James, Epistle of Barnabas, and the Book of Thomas the Contender, to name several examples. Some of these manuscripts were quite popular among early groups of Christians; but because they did not agree with the Rome-empowered, orthodox beliefs, they were not included in what would eventually become the Bible or its New Testament. One could surmise that the messages such writings contain were, therefore, silenced in order to strengthen Orthodox Christianity's influence.

After Roman Emperor Constantine's conversion to Christianity in 312 AD, it is believed that one of the earliest known references to the Bible dates to about 331 AD, when the Emperor himself requested fifty Bibles to be created by scribes for the grand churches he was constructing. Yet, we do not know what Christian texts were contained in this book. It would be decades before the books, contained in the Bible we know today, were agreed upon and officially canonized by the leaders of Orthodox Christianity. The initial request for Bibles by the Emperor followed on the heels of the Constantine-guided Council of Nicaea, the first of many subsequent councils instrumental in establishing an Orthodox Christian state religion with the same ideals. Roman government influenced the establishment of core doctrines for the Christian religion it desired, in order to affect their ever-expanding empire of people. Before the Nicene Council, Orthodox Christianity did not possess a Bible or many of the common elements of the modern-day church. It lacked structure, though regional churches and bishops had already been established. These bishops, however, did not all share the same opinions of the faith. Many attempts had been made, prior to the Council of Nicaea, to unite beliefs and bring adherence to the same legalistic doctrines within Christianity.

We can assume that the first book to attempt to be used as a tool in organizing Christian beliefs was *The Didache of the 12 Apostles* around 100 A.D., and not the Bible we know today. *The Didache* would eventually be rejected, hundreds of years later, for inclusion into the biblical canon (a list of books accepted as being Holy Scripture). This is important to mention, for it demonstrates that early Christians did not always agree on what should be claimed as the true story surrounding Yeshua. The first known attempt to form a canon of scripture, using various manuscripts, was produced in the second century by Marcion while in Rome. Being partial to the writings of the Apostle Paul, Marcion included ten letters of Paul and a form of the Gospel of Luke in his collection of Christian manuscripts. Unfortunately, he personally edited them to fit with his seemingly Gnostic beliefs. He would later be branded a heretic by Orthodox Christianity.

Many, within Christianity today, believe the New Testament Bible came into being not long after the ministry of Jesus (Yeshua), as if authors of the Bible were following the man, recording his messages and deeds. The books, that would eventually form the New Testament Bible, did not come together that easily, however. For centuries men debated hundreds of Christian texts, arguing over which writings should be considered as being authoritative and worthy for use in public reading. Early Christian leaders, such as Origen, Dionysius and Irenaeus, struggled with Christian writings because of differences of views, alterations and mistakes found within the documents, even then.

There were several reasons ancient Christian writings contained mistakes. Errors could originate with illiterate authors who had to dictate their words to scribes who recorded them. The Apostle Paul, who is credited with writing many of the Bible's epistles, for example, actually did not write very well and so employed a scribe to record his letters. If the scribe did not record Paul's words exactly as spoken, or even changed what was said, who would know? Additionally, when an author finished his literary work, he would typically make a few copies by hand and distribute them to friends or associates. This created the opportunity for more discrepancies to occur within the same manuscripts. Books were not mass-produced and took a long time to copy. There were no printing presses in ancient times. If someone wanted a copy of an author's work, they would need to hire a scribe to reproduce the writing. It was common practice for a person who received a book, to hire a scribe to duplicate it, in order to give a copy to someone else. Unfortunately, Christian texts were often changed by scribes during the copying process, or even by literate Christian leaders who made their own reproductions in order to make the writing better convey the ideas that they thought the author had implied. These examples, of purposely, altered documents, do not account for the numerous mistakes in copying that were often made accidentally. One can only imagine how many times errors within a manuscript copy would unknowingly be reproduced and coupled with additional, fresh mistakes made by scribes.

If the Bible was original and truly inspired by a Divine being, then I have several issues with this claim. Would perfect documents purportedly inspired by a supreme being ever be argued about for centuries, due to doubts of authenticity for inclusion into the biblical canon? Even more alarming is that

no original documents of any of the biblical letters
exist.  None.  If the Bible was comprised of writings
directly from God, then wouldn't such an intelligent
and capable deity make such a book incorruptible?
Furthermore, none of the Bible manuscripts are even
copies of the original writings.  It was a common
practice of scribes over hundreds of years to copy
texts, intentionally altering copies in order to attempt
to clarify meanings or make them more relevant to
cultural issues of the day.  Their manuscripts often
contained errors, as I mentioned, making the copies of
the copies of the copies we have left today definitely
not mistake-free, or even close to being perfect.  No
original manuscripts of any of the Bible books exist,
and most all of the copies that still survive today were
made from copies of copies of copies, centuries after
the originals were written.  All of the surviving
writings contain thousands of mistakes and
intentional changes from scribes, with some passages
having never existed within the original texts.  For
example, Luke 24:51, Mark 16:17-18, John 7:53-8:12,
and I John 5:7 are just a few of some major New
Testament passages found within the Bible that never
existed in the earliest known manuscripts.  This is
because scribes added these passages many years
later to either fill in the blanks, or to record popular,
unverifiable tales of Jesus that somehow were not
found in any of the texts.  So, many errors do persist
within the pages of the Bible, and there is no way for
us to know what words and meanings the original
documents actually contained for certain.  Even more

disheartening is that all four of the Gospels of the New Testament were written probably thirty to sixty years after Yeshua's earthly existence, and none of them were likely penned by the men whose names are used in their titles. Additionally unsettling is the fact that as Christianity grew in popularity, so did the authority and fame of self-proclaimed apostles, such as Paul. Were you aware that it was a common practice in that day for some to write letters in another's name in order to instantly gain credibility and an audience? For example, some of the writings attributed to Paul are believed to be forgeries, written by other, unknown authors! How can we ever deduce what was originally written within the Bible, and who for sure authored any of the books?

Having touched upon many of the errors found within the New Testament of the Bible, surely the Old Testament remains a pure work, correct? Not true at all. Let's look at but one manuscript within the Hebrew Bible, or Old Testament. The first five books are known as the *Pentateuch* and considered by some to be the most important work within the Hebrew Bible. Many believe that the first book of the Bible, *Genesis*, contains original stories. However, some of the accounts recorded by scribes thousands of years ago were most likely borrowed from ancient Sumerian texts which pre-dated *Genesis*. Sumer is one of the earliest cultures from which we have a written record of their civilization. Their religious writings in clay have survived 5000 years and most certainly influenced other religions, including the Judeo-Christian religion. The Sumerian religion was comprised of temples, priests, rituals, feasts, celebrations, lamentations, and hymns. Their gods were believed to prefer justice and mercy but also brought judgment and punishment upon people. Sound familiar? In Genesis, some of the story of the creation, as well as the Garden of Eden, was certainly borrowed from ancient Sumerian literature. For example, in the Sumerian myth *Enki and Ninhursag*, similarities can be drawn to the Genesis' account of the creation of waters, plants and animals, a divine paradise, a rib being used to form a woman, the eating of forbidden fruit, and pain during childbirth. In another example, the ancient Sumerian myth *Eridu Genesis* tells the story of a Great Flood that befell the Earth. It would appear that many of the Genesis stories were passed down among ancient civilizations long before the first word, of the first book, of the Hebrew Bible was ever thought to be scribed.

When looking at understanding the truth concerning the books of both the Old and New Testaments, it seems fitting to draw our attention to Bible translations. By translation, I mean taking a manuscript originally written in the Hebrew or Greek languages, and translating it into another language, such as English. The problem with translation in general is that each language contains its own words and meanings. Yet, some languages contain words that convey certain ideas that do not have a counterpart within other languages. A similar word just does not exist. The Bible books were primarily translated from the original Hebrew and Greek languages. Could Bible translators with one hundred percent accuracy have effectively conveyed the original intent of the words and sentences from languages which are so expressive? We cannot be certain. Words over time evolve into meaning different things. For example, one's definition of "soon," may differ from another's definition of the very same word. Recently, I was to meet a friend of mine for dinner. He called and told me he was on his way, and thus would be arriving to meet me, "soon." Twenty minutes later, he walked into the restaurant. I had been expecting him to appear about ten minutes earlier. Our definitions of the same word (in this case "soon") differed greatly. The way we use words, as well as their meanings, both change over time. Simply open a King James Version of the Bible and compare it to modern-day language and you'll know what I mean. We no longer use words such as "thou," and "thy," for example. Furthermore, language is often a barrier of sorts in comprehending how others feel, or what they are attempting to express. I can remember having a conversation with my nephew about something which now seems trivial. But at the time, I recall him saying to me after I shared a story, "*That's me, now!*" I was caught completely off-guard and thought I had offended him, because what I heard him say was, "*That's mean, now!*" So, imagine language written down, copied, and translated from an altogether different language, not once, but numerous times. Couple this with inevitable mistakes in copying, as well as purposeful changes made to the new translation over time, and we have an altogether different meaning found within the manuscript. Original feeling and intent gets lost in translation. It's only natural that problems with language become more of a hindrance when a written letter is used as a substitute for a relationship between two parties. Isn't it easier to relate to someone in person, by being able to question their words for clarification, while witnessing the expression of their emotions? Within the imperfections of language itself lies the difficulty, inaccuracy, and fallacy of the Bible being the only perfect tool for direct communication between a god and mankind. Surely, a highly-intelligent being would have found a more perfect way to communicate with us, than using a fault-ridden, instruction manual.

The invention of the printing press in the 15th century made it so books would no longer need to be copied by hand but could be printed accurately and in mass quantity. Of course, the first book to be printed was a version of the Bible known as the *Latin Vulgate*. The *Vulgate* was created from the best known Latin translations of the time and was considered to be *the* Bible of the Roman Catholic Church. Eventually, a New Testament would be created based upon the Greek texts, and a man by the name of Erasmus wanted to be the first to do so. Using inferior manuscript copies that were roughly 1100 years removed from their originals, Erasmus produced his version of scriptures using the incomplete Greek texts and part of the *Latin Vulgate* to piece together holes found within the faulty manuscripts. By doing so, he brought the first Greek New Testament to press. Unfortunately, this would be the New Testament from which the *Authorized King James Version* of the Bible (among other translations) would use as their primary source. And subsequently, the imperfect *King James Bible* would eventually supplant the *Latin Vulgate* and be used as reference for many future Bible translations that would follow.

Looking at Bible translation further, it's been said that there are at least 220 versions of the English Bible since the 1611 King James Version was created. The King James Bible was produced, by and for the Church of England, as a way of further controlling its members through a book that appeared to have God's authoritative stamp on it. Of course, the King James Bible supported the church's doctrines. Simple mistakes can be found in this Bible translation that were not accidental at all. One example that comes to mind is the purposely misrendered word "*Easter*" for the original word "*Passover*" in the Acts of the Apostles. If the Bible contains the holy words of God, then how could translators even dare to alter the words of the Divine by removing the Jewish Passover feast from the text and replacing it with a feast most likely created to celebrate the pagan goddess, Eostre? King James translators were possibly attempting to reconcile and recruit pagans to the Church of England faith. Don't get me wrong; I like feasts as much as the next guy, but doesn't this little alteration seem to discredit claims that the Bible is God's Word? And even with such nonsense and the hundreds of translations available, we should further consider that the Bible with all its shortcomings is still not available in approximately 2,000 languages. That leaves quite a lot of people without the ability to read the word of God, doesn't it? Is God going to grandfather them into the kingdom, or will they simply be forgotten for all of eternity? Do we still wish to think that the letters of this book are truly *the* divine voice to all of mankind? It is hypocrisy such as this that has caused me to look much deeper into claims regarding the Bible's infallibility.

Such a case of closer scrutiny of biblical manuscripts did in fact occur by Oxford theologian, John Mill. It took him three decades to compare 100 manuscripts of the New Testament, documenting variations found within the texts. Within the Greek and Latin manuscripts available to Mill at the time, he uncovered over 30,000 discrepancies, from mistakes to blatant alterations, which he published in a book in the year 1707. Today, we have many more manuscripts from which to compare, and so the errors and alterations found within the volume of writings that have been discovered since John Mill's

work, are even greater a number than were
uncovered three centuries ago.

Though Christianity's claims of the Bible being a
perfect, divinely-inspired work are problematic,
another wide-spread error is also being made with
regard to interpretation of the Bible.  To me, perhaps
the biggest mistake followers of Jesus make is to
attempt to comprehend biblical texts in a literal
fashion.  In three out of the four Gospels, we read
about Jesus speaking in parables.  In fact, Matthew 13
makes it a point to clarify that the teachings of Jesus
are not be understood literally:

> "*All these things Jesus spoke to the crowds in
> parables, and He did not speak to them without a
> parable.*"  - Matthew 13:34 (NASB)

A parable is a story that contains a hidden, spiritual
truth.  Much of the Bible is written in parabolic
fashion.  In fact, teaching in parables **was** a very
common way of communication in ancient times.
But, to be sure people didn't get the **wrong** idea, we
read that Jesus confirmed to his disciples that he
shared his stories in parabolic form, so as to allow the
listener to interpret the message spiritually:

> "*The knowledge of the secrets of the kingdom of God
> has been given to you, but to others I speak in
> parables, so that, 'though seeing, they may not see;
> though hearing, they may not understand.'*"

- Luke 8:10 (NIV)

Here then, lies the issue; for many preachers and teachers within Christianity not only try and glean all of life's answers from the Bible, but they attempt to do so by comprehending, and unfortunately teaching, the passages literally. This is a major error in Bible interpretation. For when the Bible is attempted to be understood literally, it becomes a fearful and damning instrument in the hands of those who wish to convert people into believers of their religion. Converts are made through fear, not truth. Yet, during the time of Jesus' ministry, we read he addressed this problem of religious leaders attempting to convert others through damnable doctrines:

> *"What sorrow awaits you teachers of religious law and you Pharisees. Hypocrites! For you cross land and sea to make one convert, and then you turn that person into twice the child of hell you yourselves are!"* - Matthew 23:15 (NLT)

Though they may not realize it, many Christians succumb to fear. Due to Christianity's teachings, which cause people to question their eternal standing before God, they fear studying the origins of the Bible, unable to examine its authenticity, or consider spiritual interpretations of the parables found within its texts. *"If I question the Bible, which is God's word, God may judge me, because I'm challenging what He says,*" some worry. Should scrutinizing biblical passages and church teachings cause one to fear such a practice may produce eternal consequences? Where is the freedom in believing such nonsense? Yet, many Christians today are content in misinterpreting much of the Bible literally, remaining blind to the fears that the good book and church doctrines have birthed within them.

If you do not yet realize that the Bible is interpreted many different ways by Christian church leaders, then simply look across the United States and recognize the numerous denominations. For the most part, they are the product of differences in Bible interpretation. How many different denominations and church buildings will it take for modern-day Christians to finally realize they are divided, being separated from one another by their beliefs? They are lost from following what they deem as being God's word, and yet do not realize that the Word of God was never a book. Even the staunchest atheist can recognize that a god capable of speaking to everyone personally would truly be divine! So, why wouldn't any of us desire to hear personal, godly direction for ourselves? Sadly, many don't - out of fear, being incapable of realizing that a relationship outside of the letter, is very freeing and most importantly, fearless.

Still it is frustrating to know that the leaders of many Christian denominations are making claims about the authority and purity of the Bible that are outright untruths. From the eyes of the listeners, it would seem completely unlikely that so many church leaders could be spewing such an abundance of misinformation. Yet, what I am sharing concerning the lack of surviving original manuscripts, the mistakes, alterations to texts, meanings lost in translation, and incorrect interpretation are all well-known and documented by true scholars of ancient writings. Christians need to take the time to consider what they are learning from Bible colleges, church pulpits, and Sunday school teachers. If they choose to do so, they may discover that what they are being taught is something far from the truth. Fear has caused many to fall asleep and become lazy in their pursuit of a higher intelligence. Followers who think they are doing God's will are, in effect, following men who are often gifted speakers, beloved, seemingly holy, but are adept at selling a convincing message, subtly adorned with fear.

Perhaps what you have been taught by religious leaders has now caused you to fear putting your Bible away. Yet, early Christians had no books from which they could read and study but relied upon hearing messages read aloud in small gatherings. By doing so, seekers of truth could listen to the messages and ponder the early ideas about Yeshua. People did not carry their Bible to church on Sunday mornings. They sought to understand wisdom through prayer and meditation, which is to say they relied upon a personal relationship with Spirit.  Allow me to clarify that the Bible is nothing more than a collection of letters that men eventually agreed should be bound together into book form; writings from others that were deemed the best fit with the doctrines Orthodox Christianity wished to promote.  What happened to all other early Christian writings that didn't find a place within Rome's plans for a Christian, state-sanctioned religion?  Regrettably, many early Christian writings containing teachings and ideas deemed incompatible were purposely destroyed or hidden away, so any opposition to the officially endorsed religion could be stamped out from within Roman society.

Looking at the Bible from another perspective, we must ask ourselves, "*Why would a god only select a few men from thousands of years ago to somehow speak to the entirety of mankind?*"  Doesn't this seem inefficient, as well as ineffective?  If a god chooses to speak to mankind through thoughts, then I should think that an all-powerful, all-knowing, loving deity would indeed want to speak personally with all people.  If you have children, would you want to speak in-person to only a select few, requiring the rest of your brood to figure out life through only the notes you left them?  Even worse, these were not your notes, but notes written by another who wishes to interpret your thoughts to your offspring for you.  If this were the case, what type of parent would you be, and what would become of your children?  Likewise, could letters written by the biblical authors ever be relevant and personal to all people and cultures in today's modern world?  How about other cultures in the world that, for thousands of years, have not had such a book to read?  It would be better that a wise, capable divine being should prefer to have a relationship with all of mankind, being able to inspire their hearts individually.  Still, a large portion of Christianity's preachers and teachers choose to turn the words of the Bible into a law for their sheep, ever guiding them away from seeking anything deeper than what their leaders can control.  Such ministers are good at telling people that the written letter of such a law is no way to please God, even citing:

> "...*for by the works of the law shall no flesh be justified.*"  - Galatians 2:16 (KJV)

Christian leaders maintain that they know this to be true.  Yet, when asked how one can know God's will, they will immediately direct their seekers to the Bible as being *the inerrant, incorruptible Word of God.*  It is within these mistake-ridden pages of collected and bound ancient texts that Christian leaders claim all of life's answers can be found.  Yet, Christian instructors are quick to point out, "*God is wise, powerful and present everywhere.*"  So, if this is indeed God's nature, why wouldn't such a capable deity simply speak to everyone personally?  An intelligent god would make the wisest, most-loving decision, correct?  Then, why would we need anyone else to hear God for us?  Why do we need letters from dead men to become our interpreter between deity and humanity, capable only of creating a pretended kinship at best?  Is this truly a personal, intimate relationship with the Almighty?  Think about it.  Can a person ever have a strong, close relationship with another based solely through written letters alone, or would one-to-one, direct communication between two beings be much better?

Christianity, in general, maintains that converts who believe in Jesus receive the Holy Spirit, and therefore do have direct two-way communication with God.  This sounds good to me, so I must ask, "Who is *your* teacher?"  I ask this, because in the Bible, we read the Spirit will reveal truth to us:

> *"When the Spirit of Truth comes, He will guide you into all truth..."*  - John 16:13

> *"Yet a time is coming and has now come when the true worshipers will worship the Father in Spirit and truth, for they are the kind of worshippers the Father seeks."*  - John 4:23 (NIV)

If we are to be taught by the Spirit, then why should we need a book or religious teachers to spiritually meet our needs?  Interestingly, the writer of I John warned people in his day not to follow men:

> *"I am writing this to you about those who are*

*trying to lead you astray.  The anointing of Spirit you possess from him remains in you, and you do not need a person to teach you…"*  - I John 2:26-27

Should Christians wish to follow the instruction found within the Bible, then I think it good for them to pay particular attention to the passages I have cited.  In fact, I understand the damnable doctrines of the religiously minded, for I was a former Bible teacher.  However, a turning point came in my life when I elected to become still and listen for guidance from within my being.  After ten years of dry Bible study, I suddenly was learning spiritual, life-changing truth almost continually.  By listening deep within me, I was purposely led away from using the Bible as my guide.  It did not happen at once, for the Bible was actually first used to show me spiritual interpretations of what I once thought were fearful passages.  Dull, archaic texts soon became alive with hidden meanings of parables being revealed.  After a couple years, the Bible was no longer necessary to instruct me, for I desired to hear what was being spoken by another *within* me.  The Bible can be used for enlightenment but only as a tool for the Spirit in revealing higher messages of truth.  It should never be held as being authoritative in any form or fashion.

Since the Bible is believed to carry the weight of God's authority by so many, let us explore briefly the ideas concerning God as portrayed within the Bible.  We are told that God is perfect and God is love.  Yet, in the Bible we see two stark contrasts of the Christian God. In the New Testament, Jesus shares with followers a god that is loving and forgiving; a parent whom he calls our *heavenly Father*. This idea of the Hebrew God, as shared by Jesus, is one of a deity desiring a personal, close relationship with the individual. Yet, the Old Testament alarmingly portrays the Hebrew god as one who is hard to appease, angry, and capable of ordering the slaughter of innocent women and children. No one in their right mind would want to be close to this deity. Could such drastic personality differences be attributed as being the same God? One should think not, for if God is perfect, then he is unchanging. In fact, the Bible says as much:

> *"For I the Lord do not change..."* - Malachi 3:6

If God is incapable of changing, why would the same god of both the Old and New Testaments vary so dramatically? Can there be two gods, or has man created two gods by accident in literature? If God is unchanging, then a God of Love, cannot be a God of Fear; neither can a God of Life, ever become a God of Death; nor a God of Truth find it possible to ever become a God of Lies. The Bible's contradictions concerning God's nature is a red flag that men have erred in creating their book-based theology. How can the Bible be God's perfect word, when the God revealed in the book has different natures? God's multiple-personality disorder was created when Orthodox Christianity sought to make the Hebrew Bible God the God of Christianity.  By combining the writings of both Judaism and Christian authors into one book, they were unable to reconcile many of the differences (such as the problem with God's nature) found within the biblical manuscripts.

Should you need any further proof that the Bible is certainly not the *"Word of God,"* then maybe I should share what the Bible itself says *is the Word*.  John Chapter One is an interesting read, and I am especially glad for the first verse:

> *"In the beginning was the Word, and the Word was with God, and the Word was God."* - John 1:1 (KJV)

Did you notice the last few words of the text?  *The Word* is God.  If we read further in this chapter, we will learn that *the Word* is *the Spirit*.  It is the *Spirit*, we are told, that *"became flesh and dwellt among us."*  And so, *the Spirit* is the *Word of God*.  God does speak to all and does so through the Spirit.  God is the Spirit; and you *are* spirit.  Spirit is the life-giving energy that encompasses everything.  That *is* relationship; knowing my spirit is one with *The Spirit*.  It is this unbreakable connection that brings *the Word* to me, from within.

In conclusion, if the Bible is God's only way of

relating a plan of salvation to humanity, then we are all in dire trouble. For should we surmise the Bible is a perfect work, being the Word of God to use as an instruction manual in order to escape eternal wrath, then God has let us down and made a huge blunder. Containing errors due to illegitimate authorship, purposeful alterations, mistakes in copying, and lacking correct interpretation through cultural and linguistic differences, the Bible is far from being a pure work commissioned by a perfect God. In fact, an almighty God without blemish would never have authored such an imperfect work; for a God who is flawless could never reveal his perfect will to a supposedly defective people through such a faulty book. If we choose to believe that the words penned within the pages of such an indecipherable puzzle are mankind's sole eternal hope for redemption, then the Christian God would certainly be unreliable and replete with trickery.

# 3  Sin & The Visible Me

When I would go to church, my motivation for doing so was to be forgiven of my sins.  I wanted to ensure my eternal fate was a good one by begging God for my forgiveness.  Certainly, I once believed that by accepting Jesus as my savior that he would bear all my sins, being punished in my stead upon a cross of crucifixion.  Though I was told I would be saved eternally for accepting Christ's atonement, I still did not feel like I was free.  Scriptures were quoted to me stating that I needed to confess my sins to be forgiven; but, I was also taught that Jesus already saved me through his shed blood, being a human sacrifice for my sins.  So, I found myself confused.  Somehow, the teaching of salvation from sins seemed hollow, scripted; and well when you add the whole blood-thing in there, very pagan.  Believing such things put me on a sick carousel of thinking, "I'm saved.  I slipped up; better confess so I'm surely saved.  Now, I'm forgiven.  Oops, I'm not forgiven," over and over.  Could I lose my salvation by the sins I did this week, or would it be from the errors I am sure to commit in the future?  I wondered what the truth was, as I was not feeling any better about my eternal security.

I previously mentioned that I posed my questions concerning Hell to both a Baptist and a Wesleyan, both being from very contrasting denominations within the same Christian religion.  The Wesleyan began citing examples of violations that would land one within the flames of Hell.  He told me if women wore short skirts, make-up, or listened to rock and roll music, they were going to Hell. If a man swore, smoked, or drank alcohol, he too would be spending eternity in the fiery nether regions. Being shocked and frankly, frightened, I happened upon a Baptist minister who told me all I had to do was accept Jesus as my personal savior, and I would be eternally secure. It didn't matter if I went out and murdered someone one after my conversion, as I was a shoo-in up in Heaven. That sounded much nicer to me, so I chose the latter denomination's teachings for me to follow. Still, I marveled how two different Christian church denominations could have such contrasting views concerning sin and the afterlife? One thing was clear: one of them was certainly incorrect; and though both of them were very knowledgeable in their specific church doctrine, most likely both were, in effect, clueless as to the truth. In my mind I knew both men were essentially guessing the responses to my questions. They were literally divining their answers through use of a book. Yet, their fate, as well as the fate of others, I was to believe hung in the balance. Through this experience, I became acutely aware that religion, especially most forms of Christianity, can do more damage than good, especially when it promotes fearful doctrines that are cited as being truth. Even if a church doctrine is plainly illogical, many Christians are simply unable to see it as such.

As my previous story pointed out, sometimes

Christian doctrines contradict one another, as they may vary from one denomination to another. A denomination is a religious organization whose members are united in shared beliefs and practices. Many followers within them have no idea where these beliefs came from or even care if they make sense. They pride themselves in being able to repeat such teachings to others, believing they are saving them for eternity. But, in fact, many Christians are more often harming people by creating falsehoods that must one day be overcome.

Let's think about sin and separation from God. If one believes they are saved from their sins, but still sees God as being separate and in Heaven, are they truly saved? In church, I was taught that my sin separates me from God. This is partially correct; because if I choose to believe incorrect thoughts produced by my ego, I will see myself as being separate from God. In fact, the very idea that God is disconnected from me and existing up in a Heaven somewhere is by definition *separation*. This idea of separation from God, the Divine Spirit, is what many believe to be true. When I look externally for answers, everything appears to be separate, one thing from another. We struggle as people to try and connect with what we see with our physical eyes, as we are social creatures by nature. Consequently, we try to understand the invisible spirit realm the same way, thereby creating in our minds a god who reigns over us from somewhere up in the heavens. But, God is not something that can be defined as "up there," or even "in Heaven." The word *god* itself creates the idea that we are indeed separate from Spirit. The truth, however, is that what we may call "God," is really the living consciousness, *or Spirit* - the all that everything exists within:

> *"God is Spirit..."* - John 4:24

> *"For in Him (Spirit), we live, move and have our existence."* - Acts 17:28

We are spirit, and part of the whole that is *Spirit*. In that sense, we are already connected with Spirit, but many live their lives unaware. Yeshua (Jesus) proclaimed this very idea and was persecuted for it when he said, *"I and my Father are one."* He knew he was one with Spirit, and likewise, all of us are one with Spirit, too. Do we really *know* this? If so, then we no longer should think of ourselves as being separate from our source and in need of being saved from the wrath of a vengeful deity who awaits to greet us with eternal punishment. When we "remember" who we truly are, we choose to mentally re-connect with our inner source. One may choose to look at this as reuniting with Spirit, the true meaning behind "re-member." By doing so, sin can no longer be understood as a word describing separation from God. We are never separate, but always united with Spirit. If we choose to believe the contrary is possible, then our false beliefs will certainly appear to be true, though they are not.  Know that separation can only occur in the fearing mind that self-creates it.

The fall of man into sin, we are taught, occurred in the Garden of Eden when Adam and Eve took a bite of an apple from the tree of knowledge of good and evil. Many Christians believe this to be where *original sin* entered the world.  And this passage does indeed tell the story of the condition of mankind with regard to sin, especially when we recognize that sin is really just an error in judgment.  Immediately after Adam and Eve consumed the forbidden fruit, we read in the first book of the Bible that an interesting thing happened: they saw themselves not only as naked, but also decided to hide in fear from God.  Interesting we read that God is said to have asked a profound question: "*Who told you, you were naked?*"  The point of this question seems not to place blame, as much as it was to marvel that the man and woman listened to someone else's false ideas about themselves and now believed they were lacking.  This parable profoundly reveals that when we look outside of ourselves for knowledge, we find a frightening world of *duality*. This outer world displays both good and evil, and that makes us feel disconnected, alone, full of fear, and unable to see who we really are.  When we focus only on the duality taking place outside of ourselves, then the connection to our source, namely *Spirit*, seemingly feels severed, as well.  The Divine then becomes a deity separate from us and thus vengeful, ready to punish us for every mistake, as we cautiously navigate through our earthly life. What is very interesting about this passage, found within Genesis Chapter 3, is that we are told *a snake* whispered unto Eve this idea of looking outside one's self for knowledge. Interestingly, when we read of Jesus speaking about sin in Matthew 12, he proceeds to attack the religious leaders of his day by calling them "snakes." These supposed men of God were misleading people, using religion to mentally separate people from their source. By calling them snakes, was Jesus inferring that the religious leaders were doing the same deed as the serpent in the Garden of Eden? They certainly were leading people to look outside themselves in order to be more godly, by relying on ritual and their obedience to a Law of commandments supposedly from God. Yeshua (Jesus) compared the religious leaders of his day to being *"white-washed tombs full of dead men's bones."* This was an obvious picture of the religious leaders' focus being solely concerned with outward practices, having forsaken their true connection with Spirit only found within. We read that Yeshua told his followers they should first look within their hearts to Spirit, and the outer cares and desires would fall into place. So, it seems right that the snake who misled Eve in the garden could symbolically have been a religious leader. If I am correct in my assumption, then man-made religion has only furthered the idea of sin (mistakenly believing we are separate from God) since the beginning.

Adam and Eve also represent the male and female part within each person. All of us have a male-female aspect to our personalities. Within each of us is the masculine, dominant, intellectual part that not only creates, but reacts - a strong force to be reckoned with. But married to this carnal man, or as the Bible calls the "first Adam," is the submissive wife named Eve. Eve is the gentle, loving, truly emotional part that each of us have. Though Adam seemingly dominates over Eve, Eve is sensitive and feels emotions. These emotions of Eve will also lead Adam, just as strongly as Adam will try and lead Eve. This emotional pull that all of us experience is described quite well in Genesis when we are told the snake whispers to Eve in the Garden of Eden. The snake created doubt, a subtle form of fear, which motivated Eve and then Adam into believing a lie. The lie was simple and still used by most Christian institutions today: "*You are lacking.*" In other words, Christianity teaches that all are sinners; and therefore, in a condition that needs to be fixed. Certainly, everyone makes mistakes and is thus imperfect, right? Evangelical, as well as Fundamentalist Christianity both suggest that Jesus took care of our imperfect humanity by dying on the cross for mankind's sins, specifically for those who choose to accept him as their Lord and Savior. The problem with this teaching is two-fold. First of all, the idea that every person is inherently bad is not true; for all of us *are* eternally perfect Spirit. This truth about us can never change. Yes, we are perfect in Spirit, though

we may not always make wise choices while still
believing the temporary, physical world is somehow
truthful.  How could something that is already eternal
(you, me and every person) need salvation?  Those
who choose to believe they need saved in order to
escape eternal separation from God, are like dairy
farmers who for some reason purchase milk from a
store.  They do not realize they already have their
own source.

Yeshua did not teach the same message being
preached today by most churches within the
Christian religion.  In fact, his message was in direct
opposition to Christianity's idea of sin and separation
when we read he proclaimed, *"The Kingdom of God
is within you"* (Luke 17:21 KJV).  In other words,
Yeshua's message was that we should cease from
looking outside ourselves, as most religions would
have us do, and look *within* to where the Divine
dwells.  You see, the tree of life is *you*.  You are the
tree, and the life, your eternal spirit, is within and
always has been.  In the Garden of Eden, we are told
that a flaming sword was put around the Tree of Life
to keep Adam and Eve from reaching it after they
believed the lie that they were separate from God.
This parable simply shows that something fearful was
used to frighten mankind away from looking within
himself; that is to stay away from the tree.  Who put
the emblem of fear, a flaming sword, in their way?
Well, who puts the teaching of a fiery hell and a
bloody cross in *our* way today?  Is it God, or really

just the religious-minded who have succumbed to fearful interpretations of life?  Most forms of Christianity raise frightening images that unfortunately obscure the way that leads to the truth of who we are.   We should learn a very simple lesson from the story of the Garden of Eden: by yielding to fear, we decide to believe lies about ourselves.  And the person who chooses to believe lies, sins; which are thankfully correctable errors in our thinking.  Sin is self-created separation from the source, which is Spirit, the true make-up of each and every person.  When fear is allowed to have power over us, it is always lodged within our past, distracting us from the present, and causing us to misinterpret our future.  Fear is created through the outside physical environment, as the tale of Adam and Eve demonstrates, and is an emotion that makes us very reactionary to the world we see around us.  Fear is empowered by us, affecting our past, present, and future.  It is fear that wrongly causes us to be tossed about, feeling mentally out of control.

Many who are trapped within harmful religion are tormented by fears created by legalism.  Legalism within religion is simply a law, a set of rules of what one should do, or not do, in order to please a divine being.  A law is also a good way to create fear in believers of Christianity.  "*Mess up, and God is angry with you,*" we are told.  For many Christians, the Jewish Law of Moses is still in effect for them in part.  They wonder if some of those commandments should be kept, though Yeshua mentioned that to love others fulfills all of them. To most Christians, Jesus fulfilled the Law in their stead, so mankind would not have to spend eternity in Hell. However, the Jewish Law was never about eternal punishment and reward, so even if Jesus fulfilled it in some fashion, then he certainly did not save mankind from eternal punishment. Whether right or wrong, the Law of Moses was only created as a system of earthly rewards and punishments for Jewish people. It was a way to control people and maintain civic order within a society. If a Jew broke a commandment and thus committed sin, their punishment according to the Law was immediate, and not in the future after their physical body expired. The Mosaic Law was never intended to be about one receiving either good or bad fruits after death of their physical body. Unfortunately, most Christian leaders have a tendency to twist the Law of Moses into being something it was not, in order to persuade people they are sinners, whose eternal fate desperately hangs in the balance of the hands of Jesus Christ.

So, what is sin? The word *sin* means "to err," or simply "make a mistake." Mistakes are lessons as they can be learned from; thus mistakes are correctable errors. The Greek word translated as "sin" in the New Testament was used in ancient Greek literature to convey the idea of being "flawed" or "defective." In that light, all thinking that is contrary to truth is really flawed and defective, as it does not bring peace or joy. So, what is sin? Sin is thinking incorrectly about who we are. When a person thinks incorrectly, the results are suffering, and that is sin. To me, thinking that has fear as its motivator is "sin." If I choose to allow fear to motivate me, then I am "sinning;" that is to say I am thinking incorrectly. For example, if I am afraid to do something because I fear God will punish me, that is fear ruling me and not Spirit, the real me within, helping to guide me toward truth. To give power to thoughts that are fear-based is the very definition of sin...of erring. It is then ironic when people who believe they are following God actually fear punishment from the same deity. That is the religious idea of sin.

In Evangelical, as well as Fundamentalist Christianity, if I do not fear God and his righteous judgment that could possibly send one away to an eternal Hell, then I cannot be saved and certainly am unworthy to follow him. This idea that fear must be the basis for any relationship, let alone with a supreme being, is really not a healthy relationship at all. For where fear exists, so does emotional turmoil. Emotional turmoil is the result of not thinking healthily. And not thinking healthily is what we call insanity, and insanity is sin. Jesus, we are told in Mark Chapter six, began sending his disciples out to preach a simple message telling people they should "repent." To recap, the Christian concept of original sin is that all of mankind is born into this state of imperfection, thanks to Adam in Eve and their fall in the Garden of

Eden. Traditional Christianity teaches that we must accept Jesus as our Savior to be saved from original sin that occurred before we were born; but that *was not* the message the disciples of Yeshua were commissioned to spread. The message of repentance was actually very simple: *"If we want to be free from sin, then we must change the way we think."* You see the word *repent* in the New Testament is translated from the Greek word, *metanoeo*, which really means *"to think differently; to reconsider."* How perfect! The good news of Yeshua's simple message was that we could change our minds and be saved! When we change the way we think, we are healed and thus saved from our own self-created trauma; and peace and joy are our fruits. This is why Yeshua can be called the *"lamb that takes away the sin of the world."* As our living example, Yeshua demonstrated who we are and how we should live. In this way, he *"takes away the incorrect thinking of the world,"* for one day all will know the truth of who they are in Spirit.

Christianity will often wrongly cite Bible scriptures, in order to prove their teaching of original sin and everyone's need to do something about it:

> *"... every sin and blasphemy will be forgiven people, but the blasphemy against the Spirit will not be forgiven..."* - Matthew 12:31

The incorrect, religious interpretation of this passage is that the Holy Spirit will prompt people to choose

Jesus as their personal savior, and if one chooses not to do so, then they have committed blasphemy against the Spirit and will suffer for eternity if they should die in their sins. But, if we were to look at this passage closer knowing that sins are simply mistakes, then it is obvious that Yeshua's proclamation makes it clear that any and all mistakes a person can make in life will be forgiven. But, what did he mean by, *"blasphemy against the spirit?"* Each person's spirit is his own voice of truth, as the Spirit within is a piece of the whole which encompasses all that exists. Many seem disconnected from their source, the Spirit, so learning to forgive one's self for things done in the body will be an impossible task to those who are not spiritually awake. Yet, each person's individual freedom will depend upon this. Furthermore, the truth of who we really are, that being eternal and perfect, can only be known through the real inner you - Spirit. If one refuses to listen to what is real found deep within, the Spirit, then how can the path to freedom be found? And, if we ignore that which seems hidden within our very being, how will the light of truth shine upon the darkness that is our misunderstanding? Yeshua was simply pointing us to the direction each of must look toward; he was directing us to look within ourselves to connect with our source, the Spirit.

It is important I share that when one begins to hear and think differently, a decision must be made concerning former Christian beliefs. When a person first questions traditional Christian beliefs, it seems to inevitably lead to that person asking a church leader (or two) about the truths being heard within. However, when age-old, Christian doctrines are challenged, fear will often be used by most religious leaders (and followers) in an attempt to dissuade the truth seeker from continuing on the path of hearing for one's self. When the religious system of organized Christianity is threatened with the loss of converts, attacks will be made in order to stop the one questioning, as well as to prevent anyone else in the congregation from hearing and thus leaving, also. No matter how subtle or good it may appear, fear will be used as smoke and mirrors in order to frighten the sheep back unto submission. I inform you, the reader, that if you hear the truth within and speak such things to the religious, you might be called a heretic, new age, pagan, non-biblical, lost, or a dabbler in the occult. Such name-calling attaches fearful labels to a person, so other Christians will not associate with them. When we look deeper at the labels that may be attached to us, we can easily see the ploy as being a childish antic of creating fear in order to preserve an institution of incorrect thinking. Oh, those who do such things will say it is in "love" and "God's will," as they wield various Bible scriptures against you. This attack should be understood as being a natural reaction to new thought:

> "*Do not give what is holy to dogs, and do not throw*

*your pearls before swine, or they will trample them
under their feet, and turn and tear you to pieces."*
- Matthew 7:6 (NASB)

Be aware that when we think differently from
common societal beliefs, it will seem the world be
against us for a season.  If you want to be free from
the clutches of Christianity, be prepared to lose some
friendships.  I know about this first hand.  When I
began following the inner guide within me, I initially
shared my thoughts with some of my closest friends
at church.  I was so excited and knew I was onto
something but was unaware that everyone has their
own time when they too become awakened to the
Spirit within.  When one hears and follows truth,
eventually the time will come when the falsehoods of
religion begin to be exposed.  It is then likely the time
to leave organized religion behind in order to pursue
the direction of one's spiritual path.  After I left, my
friends, who were also leaders in the church, were
unable to understand, and eventually tried to "help"
me during my time of folly.  Being conditioned to the
Sunday morning ritual of attending church, we
thought it might be fun to visit another Christian
congregation on the other side of the county.  Elders
from our former church got wind and followed my
family and me, eventually warning other pastors that
we were lost heretics.  The pastors they contacted
were then afraid of us, not wanting us to visit
anymore.  Many of our friends whom we had known

for as long as a decade or better would no longer speak to us. It was a very painful time that took years for us to heal.

Religious persecution can be read within the accounts of Yeshua found within the Gospels. We read he also experienced rejection from friends and family that caused him to state,

> "...a prophet is not honored in his own land or even within his own home." - Matthew 13:57

Even Yeshua's own family didn't understand him, and people who knew him prior were unable to hear his message. He was attacked by the religious leaders of his day due to the truths he heard and shared with others. One example of this is simply amazing and detailed in Matthew Chapter four. We are told that Yeshua was led into the wilderness and tested by the traducer (interpreted as "devil" in most Bible translations). According to the *American Heritage Dictionary*, to "traduce" means to "*to cause humiliation or disgrace to, by making malicious and false statements.*" This *traducer* simply brought into question, through subtle fear in the form of doubt, Yeshua's knowledge of the truth within him regarding his divine nature. Even scripture verses from the Hebrew Bible were quoted to try and dissuade him from the knowledge of the truth. This same type of battle similarly occurs within the wilderness of our own mind when we begin to hear the Spirit's calming voice from deep within, standing in direct opposition to our ego. Additionally, I cannot help but marvel at how similar the words of this devil, mentioned in Matthew Chapter four, sounds to religious leaders who use fear in various forms to lead and control their followers. Was this battle being waged solely in the mind of Yeshua between his higher self and ego, or did he possibly receive a visit from a religious leader who argued with him using scripture? Either way, this same battle will wage within all of us sometime soon, as we work to align ourselves with the truthful voice of Spirit.

How can we begin to think differently? We need to know that there are two people within us, as Yeshua referenced when he stated,

> *"Then shall two be in the field; the one shall be taken, and the other left."* - Matthew 24:40 (KJV)

The first step toward healing is to recognize that the thoughts we typically identify as being who we are, are not the truth. This false identity was created by looking outside of ourselves for answers, by defining who we are through events and things found within the physical world. For example, people remember each other by use of names. Names quickly cause us to not only identify a person within our minds, but also to remember the mental associations we have attached to them. If I witnessed Bobby make a huge mistake when he was seventeen years old, I might choose to continue to see Bob, though now age 39, as a mistake-prone individual. That is a simple example of how identities develop. Let's say I personally made a mistake in judgment five years ago. Should I continue to be labeled by my mistake? Have I successfully moved on beyond that error in the past, or have I held it in my mind and thus identified it as being a part of who I am by carrying it with me into the present? Series of mis-thinkings, such as this, create false identities. We adopt such labels about ourselves by wrongly believing them to be true. Quite often they are placed upon us by others, but we may also believe labels to be true of other people. The result is that we live in a physical world of false identities. This false identity is called by some, "the ego." The ego we create and empower is a false person, and it desires to be in control by leading and directing our lives.

I like to think of the ego as the "visible me." The *visible me* is the character that everyone else gets to see with their physical eyes. It is the outer person that people believe I really am. The *visible me* is also the person I see reflected in the mirror each day. It has all sorts of labels attached to it to define it as being "me." It desires attention and craves affirmation. The *visible me* is the one who wants the big house, the expensive car, the designer clothes and is concerned with social status and getting ahead. It is in competition with the world, fighting, struggling to survive, and says to everyone, "*Look at me!*" Can you understand how the ego is your adversary?  Is this really you who desires these things?  Do any of these examples I have given define who you believe you are?  If so, then you may find yourself to be a shallow person who suffers inside.  I implore you to look deeper within yourself. Are you able to see how we give titles to the *visible me* such as "doctor," "professor," "owner," "mayor," etc, so others will perceive this false identity as being higher in stature?  When we identify with the *visible me* as being who we really are, we set ourselves up for a fall.  Let's consider our bodies for a moment.  Think about how we seek to fix it, heal it, decorate it, and even change it; but ultimately it will fade away despite our best efforts.  These temporal, outer things only last but a few moments in time when compared to the real you - an eternal spirit.  They truly have no lasting value in the grand scheme of things and provide only fleeting comfort and happiness.  This is such a shame because so many are not happy with their exterior appearance.  Their low self-esteem is due to their focus being solely on an illusion of who they really are.   This lower-self is but a foggy image of the real person, and a faulty one at that.  Have you looked deep enough to know your true foundation is invisible, eternal Spirit?

> *"But everyone who hears these words of mine and does not put them into practice is like a foolish man who built his house on sand. The rain came down, the streams rose, and the winds blew and beat against that house, and it fell with a great crash."* -

Matthew 7:26-27 (NIV)

Yet, the image has power, because we energize it, giving it life, and making it appear real to us. Therefore, the *visible me* is very reactionary. This alter ego is motivated only by fear, being rooted in the past, and seeks to do whatever it can to survive. This is the source of all mis-thinking, the source of where sin comes from. This way of thinking *is* sin. Yet, within each person is the Spirit; the higher, non-physical self that is connected to everything, eternally perfect, peaceful, joyful and wise. This is the real you. In contrast, the ego sees the world as being separate, disconnected and competing with it for power, recognition, and existence. It sees life as something to be feared, as it fights for survival, being primitive. It is the culmination of thoughts we believe to be true about ourselves, whatever we have identified with as "me," "my," or "mine." So, the ego is easily recognized as our mis-guided thoughts, those that have fear as the underlying motivator, always connected in some fashion to the past. Yet, the true person has everything and is alive and whole - perfect in every way. This is healthy thinking and is sanity; for what is more sane than peace within one's own being? So, when the real you is able to see the mis-thinking mind as separate and not who you really are, salvation from sin has begun.

The Bible's New Testament speaks of the *visible me* when it talks about what it calls "the flesh," which is *the physical body*, such as in Galatians 5:17:

> *"For the flesh sets its desire against the Spirit, and the Spirit against the flesh; for these are in opposition to one another, so that you may not do the things that you please."* - Galatians 5:17 (NASB)

The Spirit, who you really are, is ever patient and awaiting for us to awaken to the truth of who we are; and the truth is that we are Spirit eternal. Even though one awakens to know this, the *visible me* continues on its path to try and maintain its existence and control. It seems that one cannot destroy the ego. Simply take comfort in knowing we can at least recognize its skillful method of operation. The *visible me* wants us to look outside ourselves for answers, but the Spirit desires we look within. This is the battle ensuing within us that, at times, can be most frustrating. Yeshua is quoted as having said,

> *"Truly I say to you, everyone who commits sin is a slave to sin."* - John 8:34

When we mistakenly believe that truth can be found outside of ourselves, then we are choosing to be externally guided through our five senses and brain. By doing so, we permit ourselves to be tossed about by the chaotic physical environment. This is the pathway to sin, that is to say, judging life incorrectly and reacting according to what one perceives from the outside-in.  You see, Yeshua mentioned we have a choice in Matthew 7:13-14, when he described the narrow path that few find which leads to life.  When the *visible me* is in control, it motivates a person through emotion, especially fear.  Yeshua plainly pointed out that slavery is occurring when we are subject to this mindset.  It is more than just a wrong thought; it is the entire process we can subject ourselves to, allowing reaction and incorrect judgment to become our master.  For this reason, he gave figurative examples of the *visible me* needing to be removed from being our sole guide through life:

> "*If your hand is causing you to stumble, cut it off!  It is better for you to enter life maimed, than having two hands depart to suffering a trial by fire.*"  - Matthew 18:8

When we choose to allow the *visible me* to externally lead us, we put ourselves in a place of suffering and subject ourselves to undergo trials.  These trials will perpetually challenge our choice of thinking, as we are in a sense swimming upstream instead of identifying with the inner, peaceful Spirit.  It is better truly, to seek direction and truth from within, listening to the gentle voice of sanity that resonates within everyone's being.  All are accountable to this voice; there is no escape from it as the *visible me*, being illusionary, will one day pass away.  When truth is set before us, we are accountable to choose change, and we are held so by our true self, the Spirit.  The quiet

Spirit, hidden as a gem within the rough, will not allow us to have peace. For the *true me* wants to be set free, manifesting outwardly and interacting with all. Accountability to such a change was emphasized by Yeshua when he had this to say about the religious leaders of his day:

> "*If I had not come and spoken to them, they would not have sin, but now they have no excuse for their sin.* - John 15:22 (NASB)

If sin (incorrect thinking) was by definition all the wrong things we do, Yeshua would not have been able to say the religious "*would not have sin.*" All people make errors in judgment, mistakes. Yeshua was declaring that when the sinful man, the *visible me*, is revealed to us as being separate and not who we really are, a choice needs to be made. When the truth of the two people at war within is understood, a person may either choose to continue down the same path of error or decide to embark upon an inner journey of listening to the inner guide and thus begin to wrest control away from the ego.

How does mistaken thinking trick us? It does so by primarily using the memory to hold onto our past. It is interesting that the Greek word used for *tomb* in the New Testament of the Bible is the Greek word, *mnemeion*, which means "a place of remembrance." In this way, the memory is connected with the past and with something dead, for we bury things that are lifeless within tombs and graves. Furthermore, we need to remember that our past is illusion, and so is the future. Many people choose to live in one or the other, but all we truly have is *now*. The ego relies on the past, so our false identity of who we believe we are may slant how we perceive today and the future; all based upon such past thinking. From this perspective, know that hope is a form of fear. Though hope can be somewhat positive, it only looks to the future and not *now*, being created by the ego in order to distract from the present. Understand that the ego, the *visible me*, operates like a talented magician who is very skilled in misdirection. Through a fearing mind, the ego is responsible for creating condemnation, guilt, worry (anxiety), doubt and even anger within us, which are all forms of fear produced by emotional reaction to the outer world. These feelings *are not* an angry god convicting a person of their faults, as some Christian teachers would have us to believe but simply the self-produced product of a person who leads their life solely from the outside-in. Life is meant to be lived from the inside-out, however, for the *true you* is Spirit that always strives to point us home toward what is real and thus what is true. As it can do nothing to the contrary, our divine, perfect spirit may seem like God outside of us pointing out the faults of the false, *visible me*. That is what light does; it shines into darkness which is our lack of understanding and reveals it as error in thinking. It does this so we may elect to change our mind, which is to *repent*, and thus follow the Spirit within. If it is easier, one may choose to consider the voice of Spirit within as maybe a "gut feeling," "instinct," "our source," an "inner guide," one's "higher self," "energy," or something similar. It does not matter. The idea is to look to our deepest center of existence for direction, then follow it.

So, from where does the *visible me* come? It is created by us through the great power of the mind. Each person begins creating this false identity from birth. Have you ever observed a newborn baby? One of the most interesting things to watch is when the young child begins to see his or her hands for the first time. The baby rotates his hand around, looking at all sides and angles of it, eventually coming to believe, "*This is me.*" Do you understand how it begins? As a child grows, he or she relies upon the outside world for help. An external mother and father provide nourishment, and clothe the child. The young person learns that the world is external, and not within, as the individualization process progresses. Things are separate from one another, and pain is experienced for the first time. The five senses of the child become awakened and the attachment to the outer world is further experienced. Each exterior observation of the world verifies to the child that the physical environment must indeed be real. Every additional external experience that happens to a person only serves to further mold and shape the identity of the *visible me*.

I once made a mental note of the wrong idea of
*becoming* something.  Have you noticed that children
and teenagers are often asked to consider *what they
want to be* when they grow up?  Perhaps, we should
not ask this question to young, impressionable minds.
Such a question suggests that we need to create and
become a certain identity.  People often ask
themselves, "*What do I want to be?*"  It would be
better for us to ask, "*Who am I, and what am I to do in
life?*"  If we know who we are, we might not be so
quick to lose sight of our true life path.  It is quite easy
to see how adulthood may only further cement the
idea that the illusion of false identity is somehow real.
All of this conditioning of believing the *visible me* to
be real occurs quickly during childhood and
continues into adulthood until the awareness of one's
connection to their source is lost for a season, as far as
the knowledge of it.  When one eventually remembers
their unbreakable connection with their source, that *is*
that person's salvation and an awakening has
occurred.

Know this: you are eternal, for you are of the eternal
Spirit.  Do you believe you were created?  Your body,
the *visible you*, was indeed created; for it began and
therefore must have an end.  The real question is not
whether the body was created, but *who* created it.
Something that has a beginning will have an ending;
but truth is eternal.  It has no opposite, for something
false only appears as truth temporarily; for it can
never be real.  If something is true, then *it is*; meaning

it is impossible for truth to ever have any real opposition.  Anything that might appear as opposite is illusion, for it is temporary.  Truth is, therefore, real, eternal, and can never change.  So, when you look outward into the physical world, what do you see? Maybe you see your reflection in the mirror; or another person sitting nearby.  Perhaps when you look around you see nature, or possibly a man-made car or house.  All we see with the eyes are non-eternal things that are passing away.  And, if all the things we see are passing away, then they are not truth, and therefore must be illusion.  Do you wish to base your entire life path on an illusion?  Consider that trusting a chaotic, defective environment as one's guide borders on insanity.  Can the things of temporary illusion ever produce something that completely satisfies one's eternal soul?  And, can Christianity based upon this same illusion ever deliver true joy, peace and wisdom, which is life?

Christianity would have us believe that salvation occurs when we accept that Jesus died in our place on a cross to save us from our sins.  As previously noted, Christian leaders promote a blood sacrifice as being necessary for mankind to be redeemed from sin.  To believe the cross of Jesus is the punishment that all of mankind deserves to suffer is a lie.  The mind thinking incorrectly creates the ego, believing it deserves punishment to appease a vengeful, blood-thirsty god.  Although the mind that empowers the ego, the *visible me*, creates suffering and death, it does want to survive, so it must also produce a plausible solution to this problem. The religious, fallen mind will typically find a way out of eternal punishment. The problem with believing a way out is necessary is that it never allows the mind, enamored with the ego, to truly feel safe and unthreatened. And so, the temporary belief of finding safety eventually becomes a nagging feeling of being unsafe, and a cycle of suffering through doubt is set in motion. This perpetual cycle of self-created sickness will continue until the idea of an external, vengeful deity, which permeates the fearful mind, ceases to exist. If God were outside of us and separate, this belief in punishment might be true. But the pure Spirit, call it God if you will, is within every person; and every person is spirit within *the* Spirit. What does the cross really teach us? The cross teaches us that if the *visible me* appears to be destroyed, the real me can never be harmed or threatened. The real, unseen person lives on, being Spirit and therefore eternal. Yeshua knew who he truly was, and thus did not fear death of the physical body, or death of the person his persecutors thought was a finite man. The finite man, the *visible me*, is not who *I am*. It is simply an illusion that deceives many who walk the Earth. This is most likely why Yeshua asked the question, "*Who do you say that I Am?*" in Matthew Chapter 16. After explaining that other people believed Yeshua was this person or that, Peter then answered, "*the anointed.*" That reply was the only revelation Peter needed to know about Yeshua and himself. We are anointed too, for all of us *are* Spirit.

The idea of judging one's self (and even others) is a form of punishment that the *visible me*, or our false identity deems as necessary.  Thoughts that seem to validate punishment come from misunderstanding, having evolved out of our own inner fears.  Even our societal systems of laws came out of man's inner struggles with the ego and the idea that there must be a right and wrong, a good and bad, and thus a reward and punishment.  Mankind as a whole, seeing things from only an externally-driven, fearful perspective, seems only capable of making sense by demanding punishment for wrong doing.  We try to punish ourselves until we feel we have paid the price.  Many religions, but thankfully not all, rely upon this sick cycle to gain and maintain converts to their organizations.  Through the fearful mind, guilt is produced, a prison of the mind created with seemingly no exit.  The more we search for a way out of our emotional prison cell, the more lost we become.  We find it difficult to comprehend that by believing the lies of the ego, we have created this mess and could easily walk right out of it at any moment.

Many people who struggle with self-condemnation naturally search for relief from their temporary insanity.  They typically run to the nearest church which sells the medicine, so it is believed, for their ailment.  Yet, no matter how much of this bitter pill they consume, still the sickness quietly survives like a hidden cancer within, ever threatening to one day rear its ugly head. The cure sold to most Christians, advertised by snake oil salesmen as the only magical potion one might ever need, is incapable of healing the suffering. You see, true inner peace can never be found within traditional Christian religion, as it steers us away from understanding the truth of who we really are, pushing us to believe we deserve punishment, a product of the *visible me*.

In this temporary world of right and wrong, punishment does teach lessons. For example, if one chooses to run into a wall face first, then the lesson to be learned is that the choice to do so creates a bloody nose. The person who chooses incorrectly will continue to suffer from a bloody snout until a decision is made to no longer run into walls face first. In this example, we might call choosing incorrectly, "*sin.*" So our mistakes in thinking do create pain and suffering, especially guilt, doubt, worry, condemnation, anger, etc; and all mental trauma is rooted in fear. Maybe we should look at the times in our lives when we choose incorrectly as opportunities to learn lessons which will help us choose wisely in the future. If our choices were always made through love, then fear would no longer be our motivator in choosing incorrectly. It seems all negative behaviors are choices that we can trace back somewhere to fear. Therefore, sin is fear and in opposition to knowing truth.

Yeshua, we read, pointed out that sin is never founded upon truth when he confronted his accusers by saying, "*Who out of you convicts me of sin?*" Apparently, none of the religious could detect any error with Yeshua's words, so he further questioned in John 8:46, "*So, if I am speaking truth, why are you not believing me?*" If what Yeshua was saying was correct, then he must have spoken truth. So why did the religious leaders of his day refuse to hear his teachings, and thus choose to continue to think incorrectly? Unfortunately, people have a habit of willingly closing their minds to truth, especially when it threatens current beliefs, social status, or for that matter anything to which they have attached their personal identity. We ultimately choose our own condition through what we allow ourselves to believe is true.

As sin is simply error in judgment, it is worth noting that some of our mistakes in thinking truly evolve out of how we perceive our fellow mankind. As people, we have a tendency to be hard on others, not understanding that we are eternally connected to them. All of us are one Spirit, being a part of the whole energy. What impacts one, affects the whole. Everyone has many lessons to learn on the life-journey. Understand that the wrong decisions people make are ultimately produced from correctable mistakes in thinking. Wrong decisions can indeed teach life-lessons, so we need to allow others the chance to learn. Knowing this, we should be patient with one another. For these reasons, Yeshua taught that we should forgive others their faults "*seven times seventy*" (Matt 18:21), and that we should not judge others when he declared,

> "*Don't judge, and you will not be judged. For with the same judgment you use, you will be judged also. For what measure you use, will be used against you.*" - Matthew 7:1-2

The Greek word rendered in the Bible as "judge" and "judged" is better translated as "decision." Yeshua might have said it this way, "*For what decision one decides against another, will be the decision one makes against one's own self.*" How we think is up to us. It is always our choice. Deciding to love others by recognizing our oneness in Spirit and not fault-finding, will ultimately maintain peace within ourselves. We need to recognize others as perfect extensions of Spirit. Otherwise, when we choose to attack others, we truly attack ourselves by producing guilt, a form of subtle fear, that hides within us. We assault others because we often falsely believe the ego's lie that we are elevating our own self by doing so. Our conscience will quietly point out this error in thinking, and we will in-turn create for ourselves guilt and condemnation from the same fear that produced the wrong decision in the first place. We may not hear the voice now as we live our lives, but one day this "judge" will bring to remembrance the things we have done against others when we chose to think incorrectly. Our judge cannot allow us to be free from the prison we create for ourselves, until we deem we have paid the full price for our errors. The price is to simply see life differently, a true change in our thinking. We read Yeshua said,

> *"Settle matters quickly with your adversary who is taking you to court. Do it while you are still with him on the way, or he may hand you over to the judge, and the judge may hand you over to the officer, and you may be thrown into prison."* -
> Matthew 5:25 (NIV)

He further tells us that we will not escape this prison until we have paid the last price. In this parable, we are the adversary, not another, with whom we may have differences. The judge is simply our conscience, the Spirit within, who will not let us stray far from truth. This judge quietly points us back to truth in all things, never meaning to condemn us. This voice, though it sometimes may appear to be silent, is ever present within us, shedding light on the path that will lead us back to truth. In the New Testament, the word traditionally translated as *judgment* is the Greek word *krisis*, where the English word "crisis" is derived. A crisis is best described as being *a decisive moment.* This is good to know; for when we read Yeshua said, *"Every careless word that people speak, they will think about in the day of crisis"* (Matt 12:36), he was referring to the time of decision we must all come to eventually. When we finally realize that our own mental mistakes can be corrected by simply thinking differently, then our *crisis* of cerebral trauma will end and peace will be known. In that sense, when we make the conscious decision to think correctly, the *crisis* certainly becomes a significant event - a pivotal change in a person's life.

Condemnation and judgment are always self-created and never an act of God. In fact, we read in the Bible that Yeshua did not judge (John 8:15), or condemn any person (John 3:17, 8:11):

> "*Do not judge, and you will not be judged; and do not condemn, and you will not be condemned; pardon, and you will be pardoned.* - Luke 6:37 (NASB)

In the above passage, pay close attention to what it says: (You) do not judge, and you will not be judged. (You) do not condemn, and you will not be condemned. (You) forgive, and you will be forgiven. This verse never mentions a god doing the judging, condemning or forgiving, now does it? It's a simple message, but profound, correct? We need to be quick to forgive ourselves and others if we do not wish to suffer needlessly. True forgiveness can be defined as learning to forget the mistakes we make, as well as the mistakes of others. Forgiveness is putting one's self in another's shoes and understanding that all of us are leading lives that are at times mis-directed.  Our perspectives, the vantage points from where we are able to comprehend life, may differ; perhaps even being faulty, making some unable to grasp a better understanding, right now.  Yet, know that all people one day will come to understand, that is comprehend truth by knowing it, rising above living lives motivated by that which is external, temporary and illusionary.  If we can somehow live in the now, today, we are then able to leave behind our past mistakes, as well as the mistakes of others, and enjoy the moment.  Know that we always have power to choose what we believe, and these choices eventually produce what we experience.

# 4  What the Hell?

When one thinks of "hell," the word itself brings up connotations of demons tormenting people in a place of fire for all eternity.  This Christian idea of Hell, however, was not accepted by some of the religion's earliest leaders and was never a doctrine of Yeshua (Jesus).  Over time, the teaching of a fiery place of punishment for the wicked became adopted as official church doctrine.  Hell was further embellished over the centuries by various Christian leaders, authors and preachers, and still today is being used by Christians as the primary method to win converts over to Christianity through fear.  The harmful concept of eternal punishment was created by men of religion, and furthered through incorrect interpretation of Bible verses.  It will be important for me to summarize the emergence of Hell in church doctrine, as well as use some Bible passages to help undo the damage caused by such fearful teachings.  I often find it enlightening to investigate the Bible in order to negate the fear that was initially created through its misinterpretation.  We will also expose errors in logic that the belief in Hell creates.  By doing so, hopefully I will be able to help those who have fallen victim by believing Christianity's teaching of an eternal Hell.

The Christian practice of suggesting an eternal place of punishment has created a large amount of frightened people, but has helped no one.  Those who choose to believe in an eternal Hell typically think that when a person dies, the soul either ascends unto Heaven or descends into everlasting fire.  This traditional, Christian idea allows for no other option (Catholicism's purgatory teaching aside): everyone will one day either be in a place of peace Christians call Heaven; or suffer for eternity in a fiery place deemed as Hell.  We are told to believe that the doctrine of Hell was taught by Jesus, who most Christians claim is God.  If believers claim God said, *"Hell is real,"* then we learn it must be so.  Christianity furthers this message of fear by telling tales of a Devil and his brood of demons who are supposedly wreaking havoc upon the world; who eventually will suffer in the same Hell as punishment for their deeds. Purveyors of such myths simply use fear to keep people from ever considering anything contrary to their teaching.  If we should challenge God's word, that would be considered heretical.  When these teachings are examined, however, it is quite easy to see they are erroneous, fear-based, and therefore incapable of bringing peace to anyone who believes such damnable heresies.  Yet, many believe the Christian fable of Hell, because they were told to do so by family, friends, or acquaintances; fearing repercussion by God, fellow church members or family should they believe differently.  If the majority of a society believes something, we believe it must be true.  Why do we feel like we must follow along with societal beliefs, never considering that their way of thinking could possibly be wrong?  Let us challenge what so many believe to be real by looking closer at how Hell was invented and why.

First and second century Christians were not found in church buildings.  There was no Bible, offering plates, pulpits, programs or stained glass windows.  People met in small groups, whereby varying beliefs concerning Yeshua were bantered about and eventually spread.  Interestingly, Clement of Alexandria (150-215 AD), considered an early Christian church father, never mentioned an eternal Hell and apparently taught universal salvation of all.  Also, Origen (185-254 AD), another prominent, early church father who wrote commentaries on nearly every manuscript later included within the Bible's New Testament, believed all of mankind would be reconciled and that no one would suffer in an eternal Hell.  Furthermore, even the earliest doctrinal statements, such as the Apostles Creed and later the Nicene Creed (325 AD), never taught an eternal place of punishment for all of mankind.  However, other early church leaders such as Tertullian (155-222 AD), a lawyer turned Christian, did write about the eternal punishment of the soul.  So, the idea of an everlasting place of punishment was believed by some early Christians but as only one interpretation within Christianity's varied beliefs.  A few early Christians believed in the eventual annihilation of all wicked people and not perpetual suffering.  Still, by the fourth century, many prominent church leaders noted that the majority of Christians at that time believed all of mankind would be reconciled – that none would be lost to eternal suffering.  The Orthodox Church was becoming pretty well organized by the fourth century, but it had its work to do if it was going to change popular beliefs.  How did the teaching of eternal punishment overpower the more prominent belief in the complete reconciliation of mankind?  The idea of Hell was strengthened over hundreds of years through promotion by religious leaders within a government-empowered Christianity.

As I mentioned in the previous chapter, Roman Emperor Constantine was an Orthodox Christian convert who exercised his leadership in order to organize and strengthen Orthodox Christian ideas.  This form of Christianity would soon become powerfully energized, becoming the preferred state religion of Rome in 379 AD.  He likely envisioned expanding the growing Orthodox Christian view, in order to unite and control his empire.  There were different ideas regarding Yeshua and his teachings at the time, so Constantine formed and presided over the Council of Nicaea in 325 AD, seeking to establish core Orthodox beliefs.  Even though there were other influential men and various attempts to organize Orthodox views prior to Constantine, it was the Roman Emperor himself who would have the power to rectify differences in beliefs between Orthodox bishops.  This statement of beliefs is now known as the *Nicene Creed*, a profession of faith that would be given high importance within Orthodox Christianity, especially Roman Catholicism. How did Constantine's group of religious supervisors arrive at an agreement concerning their beliefs? Orthodox bishops who disagreed with the Nicene Council's consensus were simply excommunicated to create unanimity. This first Council led to many other Council meetings that took place over hundreds of years, which further decided what was to be of the faith and what was to be tossed out. It is important to reiterate that Christianity was not formed by Yeshua, but the religion was created by men who came after him. Over centuries, doctrines were formed and anyone or anything that stood in the way of the Orthodox Church's plans were either removed, destroyed, or banished. Diverse groups of early Christians and their ideas were eventually silenced, even persecuted until they no longer existed. Then, Orthodox Christianity simply claimed they were the only view, essentially rewriting history. This is how the Christianity we know today began, being empowered by marrying government to religion in order to increase its influence over people. This version of Christianity became powerful and had the continuing financial support of government to grow even stronger.

Though the Council of Nicaea did not create specific doctrines concerning Hell, it is important to understand that this marked the beginning of an empowered Orthodox Christianity. Today, most all

of the denominations within Christianity can trace
their roots back to early Orthodox beliefs.
Catholicism began promoting the teaching of Hell
long before most other forms of Christianity (such as
various Orthodox and Protestant churches) branched
off unto their own direction. In other words, the idea
of an eternal Hell within Christianity was
promulgated by Catholicism, and then simply
adopted by later versions of Christianity that would
arise. By the late fourth century, Catholic Bishop St.
Augustine worked diligently to incorporate writings
from Greek philosophers (such as Plato) into
Catholicism, in order to create doctrines that would
eventually strengthen the Catholic Church's position
of power. In order to achieve this, Augustine strongly
advocated the eternal punishment of the wicked. In
fact, he maintained that unless people, including
infants, were baptized, they would go to Hell.
Doctrines such as these were not believed by every
Christian leader of the time, but Augustine's efforts
began scaring the Hell into (and certainly not *out of*)
people. It wasn't until the sixth century that the
Athanasian Creed was created which happened to
outline the fate of evil people. It was the first official
statement of Orthodox Christianity's doctrine
concerning an eternal Hell:

> "*And they that have done good shall go into life
> everlasting: and they that have done evil into
> everlasting fire.*" - *excerpted from the Athanasian
> Creed*

If the idea of Hell as eternal punishment had been subscribed to by earlier church fathers, it surely would have been clearly stated in previous official proclamations of faith, such as the Apostles' Creed or the Nicene Creed.  It took hundreds of years for the idea of an eternal Hell to be established, and the doctrine would slowly grow to prominence over hundreds of years to come.

Additionally, the idea of Hell was strengthened through various authors of the Christian faith over the centuries.  For example, portrayals of Hell can be found within the writing of Catholic, Italian poet Dante Alighieri (1265-1321), who impacted many with the *Divine Comedy*, a story of his journey through Hell, Purgatory and Paradise.  In another example, the Christian concept of Hell, being occupied by Satan and other fallen angels who were cast out of Heaven, was greatly embellished by Christian, English poet John Milton (1608-1674) in *Paradise Lost*.  Couple this with frightening messages delivered by fire and brimstone preachers and missionaries (such as Thomas Vincent, Jonathan Edwards, and George Whitefield), and the growing beliefs in hellish ideas expanded across the globe over the next few centuries.  Consequently, our common societal beliefs today concerning Hell have been strongly influenced by both Catholicism and other numerous Christian denominations that broke away from the Orthodoxy.  It took many years and many different forms of

Christianity to negatively impact the masses into fearing their potential afterlife fate.

Ancient mythologies, as well as other religions, sometimes had their versions of hell-like suffering that further influenced society's belief in future punishment. Governments took note. History reveals that beliefs in an eternal Hell were also purposely promoted by men in positions of governmental power, who felt it necessary to rule over masses of people through use of fear. Government, even in ancient times, had a purpose in working with religious leaders, and that purpose was control:

*"It has been handed down in mythical form from earliest times to posterity, that there are gods, and that the divine compasses all nature. All beside this has been added, after the mythical style, for the purpose of persuading the multitude, and for the interests of the laws, and the advantage of the state."* - Aristotle

*"The multitude are restrained from vice by the punishments the gods are said to inflict upon offenders, and by those terrors and threatenings which certain dreadful words and monstrous forms imprint upon their minds. For it is impossible to govern the crowd of women, and all the common rabble,*

*by philosophical reasoning, and lead them to piety, holiness and virtue - but this must be done by superstition, or the fear of the gods, by means of fables and wonders; for the thunder, the aegis, the trident, the torches (of the Furies), the dragons, etc, are all fables, as is also all the ancient theology. These things the legislators used as scarecrows to terrify the childish multitude."* - Strabo, the geographer

*"Since the multitude is ever fickle, full of lawless desires, irrational passions and violence, there is no other way to keep them in order but by the fear and terror of the invisible world; on which account our ancestors seem to me to have acted judiciously, when contrived to bring into the popular belief these notions of the gods, and of the infernal regions."* - Polybius, ancient historian

While digesting that Hell is a creation of religion, also consider if fear is the root of one's religious teaching, that teaching will never be based upon truth. Both teachers and followers of such fearful beliefs are unwittingly lost, yet still seek to lead others into participating with them in their insanity. Knowing that religion created the concept of Hell, and that government supported the audacious idea in order to establish more control through fear, one might wonder from where the Christian model of Hell might have been conceived. The word *hell* itself was derived from the Old English word *helan*, meaning *to conceal*. The term *hell* was originally used to describe the underworld, a place where newly departed souls go.  Interestingly, the idea of a place of fiery punishment did not completely originate within Roman Catholicism but can also be found in several early cultures.  Both the Babylonian and Assyrian religions depicted the underworld as a place full of horror reigned over by fierce gods, while Egyptian religious texts portrayed the underworld as having fire as punishment for the damned.  It is likely that these early concepts of eternal torment and fire influenced many other religions that would follow. Classic Greek mythology placed *Heaven* above, with a dungeon of torment and suffering called *Tartarus* being found below within the underworld *Hades*. *Hades* was simply the idea of an underworld place where all go when they die and not a place of eternal punishment itself.  These ancient beliefs regarding the underworld were borrowed by Christian leaders when retelling their own version of Hell.  Some early authors of Christianity included such ideas into their writings (such as the use of the word *Tartarus* in II Peter 2:4, which was likely written by another falsely using Peter's name).  Other references to Hell in the Bible, however, were either added by altering preexisting biblical manuscripts or taking liberties with language interpretation.

As the Bible New Testament was originally written in Greek, the traditional meaning of the Greek word *hades* was changed from being the place of departed souls, into a place of eternal punishment. Bible translators simply did so by translating *hades* into the word *hell*, and teaching that Hell was indeed a bad place. As mentioned previously, the 1611 King James translation of the Bible from the Greek language into English was produced for the Church of England. This gave Christian leaders a government-authorized, English Bible they could cite in support of their specific teachings, especially the doctrine of Hell and eternal punishment. The King James version of the Bible has been one of the most popular and influential translations ever produced. Its influence in expanding the idea of eternal punishment cannot be ignored. Through various tools and methods, we can see how a Christian religion of fear permeated our society, being accepted over time as a teaching of Jesus. But when examined closer, the idea of Hell could never have been what the real Jesus (Yeshua) taught or ever intended to be his legacy.

Other religions teach of trials for some in the afterlife, but in a much different way. For example, in Buddhism, one's personal hell would represent a temporary spiritual cleansing before a final restoration. Accordingly, this lines up quite nicely with the symbolic use of fire within the Christian Bible. Fire is used in the Bible to represent purification (refinement) but is almost always misinterpreted as being the flames of Hell. In the

Gospel of Mark Chapter Nine, we read Yeshua taught that torment (call it hell if you like) is our own self-creation, a condition of the mind we create for ourselves when we choose to think incorrectly. If we mistakenly think these verses are literal descriptions of Hell, by believing Jesus taught bad people are punished by God, we regrettably ignore an important sentence near the end of the same chapter: *"Everyone will be salted with fire."* Should this sentence be about the infernal fires of Hell, it would mean all of mankind must burn in a place of punishment forever. Such an interpretation wouldn't make sense, for even Christianity does not teach total annihilation of the human race. Are we all going to Hell for an eternity of torment? No, and this sentence is part of a parable that figuratively suggests our emotional trials are a *hell* we put ourselves through after making wrong choices. It is much easier to understand that our wrong decisions lead to suffering until we learn to choose differently. When we no longer make wrong choices due to misunderstanding, our suffering will cease.

If fire in the Bible is supposed to be a product of the Devil and an eternal Hell, why would God's prophet Elijah call fire down from the heavens? Furthermore, how could God (whom we also learn, in Hebrews 12:29, is a *"consuming fire"*), or his messenger, speak out of a fiery bush to Moses in Exodus Chapter Three? Are we to assume the Judeo-Christian God was in Hell when he spoke? Representations of fire, in certain passages of the Bible, are not necessarily a bad thing. It truly depends on how we choose to perceive fire. We tend to think of fire as something negative, but fire has good uses, too. Refining by fire, for example, is the process of freeing something from impurities. Refinement is a common symbol in the Bible often used to represent purification of the mind from false ideas.

One still might wonder, *"How there can be a mistake in Bible interpretation regarding fire and hell?"* I reiterate, there are two ways to interpret biblical passages: either literally or as a parable. Yeshua taught hell (emotional trauma) as being something that can take place within us. This lines up perfectly with his style of teaching. Many of his parables dealt with the inner condition of man, and so it should come as no surprise that he would use symbolic language to describe inner turmoil. This should lead us to wonder why most Christian leaders today teach that Jesus' words should be understood literally, yet still believe they comprehend the hidden messages that were shared in parabolic form. Instead of directing people to look at the heart of our issues, they steer them toward external, fearful things. And, so they believe they bring peace and love to mankind but are actually creating deeper, unseen, emotional trauma for many. It is no wonder the word hell is so misunderstood and feared by many.

In order for this injustice to be fully comprehended, I

feel I must further explain the current Christian use of fear to promote growth of their religion. Today, a majority of Christian leaders create the fear of Hell to not only enlarge their congregations but to hold people captive under their influence. Let's think about this. Such Christians generally use fear to seduce converts to their religion, teaching impending doom of eternal consequences is inescapable, unless one receives forgiveness beforehand. We learn Hell is inevitable, if we do not change our ways and accept their religion's plan of salvation from such a terrible place. Of course, such a horrible fate as Hell will not happen to the people who choose to listen to their Christian leaders and following their directives. Such promoters of fear within Christianity are like rich doctors who not only get to diagnose every patient as being sick but also reap in the profits from being the only source of medicine to cure what ails everyone's affliction! I refuse to sugar-coat what I see that is terribly wrong. Becoming prophets for profit, what many call the Christian church has truly become a den of thieves and robbers. Many Christian leaders want to enlarge their following, increase their programs, and reap the fruits of their labor while being disguised as helping people. They use fear to motivate people to follow their will, while claiming to speak a message from God in order to mask their intentions. Their brashness has grown to the point of slick media campaigns, television programs, and even modern music designed to lure as many people as possible. Many Christians unknowingly succumb to such messages of fear and then spread it like a disease to those around them. If you have inner fears created by the Christian message, you need only remember that fear is always false, man-made, and the cause of all mental anguish. Recognizing fear is then the first step in gaining one's freedom from a religion that seeks to control people:

> *"Let not your heart be troubled, neither let it be afraid."* - excerpt from John 14:27 (KJV)

Could the same man who made such a statement ever teach fearful ideas? If the sayings attributed to Jesus in the New Testament are accurate, Yeshua never mentioned a place of eternal torment or threatened anyone with Hell as punishment for not following his teachings. There is absolutely no word for such a place as Hell ever written in the original Aramaic, Greek, or Hebrew languages found anywhere within the Bible. There are, however, mistranslations into the English language of a few words from the biblical languages, especially in some older translations of the Bible. These mistranslations found in older Bibles, such as the King James Version I mentioned previously, are the only basis left for modern Bible teachers to continue to perpetuate such false doctrines. Amazingly, many newer Bible translations are leaving the word *hell* out altogether, as it just does not exist within any of the New Testament manuscripts' original language. Thus, Hell, as taught today by traditional Christianity, never existed before or during the days of Yeshua. Hell is nothing more than a myth, created by leaders of religion to control others through fear; a lie that must be undone within the human consciousness.

Allow me to reiterate, the actual word "hell" is not in the original languages that were used to write the books of the Bible. The words (*sheol* and *hades*), that were often wrongly rendered by Orthodox Christian translators as *Hell*, better meant the *"common grave of mankind - the unseen place where men go upon death of the physical body - the place or state of the dead."* Another word mistranslated as *Hell* is the Greek word *gehenna*, and it was well known in Yeshua's day as the Valley of Hinnom (a former place of idol worship turned trash dump outside the city of Jerusalem). Gehenna is indeed a literal place but one that exists on Earth and was used by Yeshua only to convey a spiritual principle. If we were to visit the region of Gehenna today, we would not find a Devil or anyone suffering fiery torment. So, *Gehenna* would best be understood as representing a suffering state of mind due to incorrect thinking - something which is surely correctable.

Not only was the word *hell* incorrectly inserted into Bible translations, but another Greek word was also incorrectly rendered in order to further establish the idea of eternal punishment. The words "forever" and "eternal" in the New Testament of the Bible are mistranslations of one Greek word used to create the fearful phrases "*eternal punishment*" and "*eternal damnation.*" The word purposely translated incorrectly as "*forever*" or "*eternal*" in most Bibles is the Greek word *aion*, which means "*a set period of time,*" meaning "*an age; having an end.*" It should be easy to understand that if something has an end, it cannot be eternal! But, by changing the meaning of *aion* ever so slightly, the idea of eternal punishment was cemented in the minds of many Christian followers. This mistranslation is especially found in the King James Bible, and as I pointed out prior, still being widely used by many today and the primary reference for many other Bible translations that would follow.

It is important to clarify that when the word *hell* is encountered within some translations of the Old Testament, it is always the Hebrew word *sheol* translated incorrectly. *Sheol* occurs at least 64 times in the Old Testament but is only mistranslated as *hell* 32 times in the *King James Bible*, while being translated as "*grave*" or "*pit*" in the remaining passages. King James Bible translators could only make the word *hell* fit into a portion of the Hebrew verses that contained the word *sheol*, but it was enough to make people believe that eternal Hell was a doctrine that originated from Judaism. However, the Hebrew scriptures are plain that *sheol* is best understood as being "*the place or state of the dead.*" It is important to know that a place of endless torment after death is not represented anywhere within the Hebrew texts, because it was never a Jewish doctrine (I recall a Jewish acquaintance once telling me she was taught that hell is on Earth!). If everyone's eternal fate is possibly in jeopardy, wouldn't it make sense that we would find at least one reference to eternal suffering in the Hebrew Bible, as well as the importance of how to escape the fiery flames? Is it not odd then that Hell was never mentioned by the Old Testament patriarchs, such as Moses or Abraham? The only way one can manufacture such a doctrine in the Hebrew Bible is through misinterpretation of a book's history (to whom was it written, for example), by incorrect translation (of Hebrew words into English), or by viewing poetic and prophetic writings as being literal. Prophetic books, such as Isaiah and Daniel, contain rich, word pictures of symbolism that should not be understood verbatim. Like the New Testament, fire is almost always used in the Hebrew Bible as a metaphor to describe human refinement, but many Christians choose to view flames as frightening descriptions of a Hell. If I were to write that a person was having a "meltdown," would you think I was describing a human being actually melting like hot butter? No. You would likely understand that the person was struggling with some emotional issues. It is easy to see from this example how we can wrongly perceive frightening things where they were never intended. And, if we look at portions of the Hebrew Bible that contain literal instruction, Hell simply is never mentioned. A place of eternal punishment is not referenced within the Law of Moses, which describes only temporary, earthly punishments for disobedience to God. Therefore, Yeshua, a Jewish Rabbi, would not have taught an eternal place of suffering that Christian leaders today would like us to believe is true.

Let's look closer at a passage attributed to Yeshua. We read in Matthew 16:18 that he said, "*The gates of Hades* (incorrectly translated as Hell in some Bibles) *will not prevail.*" We know that the word *hades* means *the state of the dead* and not an eternal place of punishment as Christianity would have us to believe, and this passage proves it. If the word *hades* meant eternal punishment, would it make sense for Yeshua to proclaim that the gates that hold people captive in an eternal Hell will one day no longer trap them? If so, how could Hell be a dreaded place of eternal suffering? Hell would not be eternal, but something temporary. Furthermore, King Hezekiah, in Isaiah 38:10, mentioned these same gates as Yeshua but used the Hebrew word *sheol* when he said, "*In the midst of my days I will enter into the gates of Sheol.*" Was Hezekiah saying he wanted to go to a place of eternal damnation, or was he perhaps envisioning the place where everyone's spirit resides after death of the physical body? Contrasting these two passages makes it very clear that Yeshua foresaw that the human condition will eventually change for the better. One way or another, all emotional trauma (hell) will be healed. To some, like the Greeks, *Hades* represents the place of the dead. But, maybe Hades best represents the state of people who are spiritually dead, having become lost souls in need of truth. The mind can become a prison whose gates shall one day need to be unlocked. Could the mind elevated out of the prison of emotional trauma and mis-thinking be the better meaning behind the idea of *resurrection?*

Such ideas beg the question, what happens when we die? Near death experiences have shown that when the body of a person expires, the Spirit lives on. Most people who have died and come back tell of seeing loved ones in Spirit who were waiting for them, having been eager to help the newly departed transition to the Spirit world. Next, a tunnel of light is typically encountered that is often best described as overwhelming, pure love. As the spirit *or soul* of the person continues through toward the end of the tunnel, there usually comes a point when a life-review is experienced. The life-review from physical birth to death, though detailed, is often said to have taken place in a mere instant. Should a person reject heading into the light, unwittingly declining the cleansing life-review, the spiritual journey does not typically continue. A decision has been made to return to the Earth plane. Such near death experiences cause me to wonder about death of the physical body. What happens to a person who wants to remain here after the body dies, but their spirit cannot return to reside within it? I think we can assume that an experience similar to the near-death scenario is potentially what occurs. If the spirit of a person does not head to the light to be with loved ones and continue the life-journey, that person likely will remain earthbound but without a physical body. By earthbound, I mean to remain attached to the earthly plane of existence. We could suppose that such a spirit would be mentally held captive to their past life. A spirit that chooses to remain behind has unknowingly chosen not to continue their life-journey, being in some form of emotional trauma, staying confined here. Do we realize how such a lost spirit could be in limbo due to prior emotional baggage? Though their time on Earth is complete, they simply do not want to leave for whatever reason. Fear would ultimately be the cause of such a condition, whether it's fear of eternal punishment, fear of loss, condemnation, guilt, doubt, worry, anger, or whatever form of fear one can imagine. This traumatic state of the lost, disembodied spirit could also be an additional interpretation of the *hades* (or *sheol*) of which Yeshua spoke. Perhaps such people in Spirit, who are lost and suffering, need *resurrected* into the light, becoming elevated through enlightenment to the truth of who they are in the divine Spirit. Knowing there is forgiveness and no everlasting punishment, some call Hell, could certainly go a long way toward helpless spirits gaining their freedom. We might choose to call such lost entities "ghosts," while most Christians would think such an idea to be impossible. Christianity generally teaches that disembodied spirits of people are permanently residing in either Heaven or Hell, not allowing for any other possible scenario. This notion differs from the Bible's I Peter, which claims Yeshua went to preach a message to deceased people from the time of *The Great Flood*:

> *"...he (Yeshua) went and preached to the*
> *spirits in prison, who had disobeyed God long*
> *ago, while He waited patiently during the*
> *time of Noah, when the ark was being built."*
> - I Peter 3:19-20

If this passage is true, then we must ask ourselves, *"Where were these people residing?"* If they were in an eternal Hell, then Yeshua would have no incentive to preach to those who were impossible to save. It is evident that Yeshua *did* want to help them. They were in need of assistance due to suffering, but their painful condition obviously was not eternal. So then, hell cannot be a place that holds people perpetually captive. I also find it difficult to believe that these poor spirits, from times long ago, needed rescued if they had been residing in an ever-blissful Heaven. That wouldn't make sense, for in Genesis we are told that God supposedly flooded the whole Earth in order to destroy these same wicked people. Most Christians believe that wicked people go to Hell, so they could not be in Heaven. Where were they, that they could be rescued from turmoil? I would suggest these lost spirits were simply trapped to this plane of existence but without physical bodies. They needed a message to help them understand truth that would set them free from their past, and Yeshua sought to deliver that to them.  By freeing them from their fears, they were able to transcend the earthly realm and continue the journey of life.  Traditional Christian theology has no real answers to such questions, and often makes little sense when explored deeper.

With or without a body, hell can only describe the state of mind trapped in fear, lost in the life journey.  It is a temporary condition, one which can be changed by love.  Fear, the root of all incorrect thinking, causes mental and emotional torment which *is* hell.  There are suffering people walking the Earth who are in a state of hell right now and in need of love.  Some of those hurting people have physical bodies, while others may just be the ghosts of those who remain trapped here with us.  I use the word "ghost" again to indicate a lost human spirit that is in need of direction, for a ghost is truly only a misguided shell of the real person within.  I find it necessary to mention ghosts, because there is never separation, and everyone is connected with one another in Spirit.  We need to understand that hell is created when people allow fear to control them, a condition which may eventually produce a false snare that seems hopeless.  Remember that all mental hell is only temporary, being a state of mind that will be corrected within everyone, no matter where they are today in life's journey.  If we believe and teach that some will suffer eternally as punishment for things done on Earth, then we are culpable in spreading a very harmful lie that causes mankind to suffer needlessly. I would rather instruct people that wrong choices affect our frame of mind, no matter which side of the grave we find ourselves. Such wrong choices are harmful but thankfully correctable errors in judgment. Correction can quickly transform suffering into peace.

Hell is false. What more proof do we need? If Hell were a literal place, then an everlasting chamber of torment would had to have been created by what's been described as being a loving God (Colossians 1:16). Take a moment to think about this: Do the words *loving* and *Hell* belong in the same sentence? If we are to believe that God created Hell to punish the wicked, as traditional Christian theology teaches, then we encounter a contradiction in the very beginning of the Bible's Book of Genesis where we read, "*God created the heaven and the earth.*" Where did Hell come from? There is absolutely no mention of a vengeful God ever creating an eternal place of punishment within the Bible. Hell, then, must be a creation of the mind of man.

Let's look at the idea of creation logically. Since many Christians believe that God is all-knowing (omniscient) and all-powerful (omnipotent), then why wouldn't such a God simply create those whom he already knew would make the choices he preferred? God would then not have to destroy anyone for making incorrect decisions. Otherwise, we would be right to declare that such a God is evil and unjust. If some people are evil, why would a shrewd god needlessly have created them? Would a good, loving, all-knowing deity ever make the decision to eternally punish people, when there was no need to ever create those whom he foreknew he would eventually destroy? Certainly, if God is all-powerful and all-knowing, he should have easily been able to design only those whom he truly desired. This would have spared the rest of us from ever existing and eventually having to face eternal wrath for making incorrect choices; all of which God knew in advance we would inevitably do. This brings another question to mind. Could a perfectly good God be capable of creating evil people? If so, then evil could not have originated from a good God. Such a god's nature would have to inherently be evil. So are we left to assume that the perfect Christian God made a mistake by creating a world of imperfect, unworthy idiots? Is that what we are to believe? If God is perfect, he would be incapable of error. No matter what scenario Christianity wishes to propose, the idea of a good God creating people that would eventually end up in Hell does not make sense. Logically, would a just God eternally punish people for making only temporary errors in judgment? I challenge you to examine what you currently believe, as any religion that teaches an eternal Hell is illogical and a cause of much mental anguish.

If you find yourself struggling with what I write, then

at least consider some Bible passages that do not agree with the idea of anyone being lost forever. The following verses are just a few that imply the restoration of all people (emphasis mine):

*"...the restoration of all things..."* - Acts 3:20-21

*"...for all shall know me (God), from the least to the greatest."* - Hebrews 8:11

*"...God, who is the savior of all men..."* - I Timothy 4:10

*"...who will have all people to be saved, coming to the knowledge of the truth."* - I Timothy 2:4

*"...that God may be all in all."* - I Corinthians 15:28

*"(Christ) was the true light which lights every man that comes into the world."* - John 1:9

*"...in the dispensation of the fulness of times he might gather together in one all things in Christ..."* - Ephesians 1:10 (KJV)

*"Call no person common or unclean."* - Acts 10:28

*"...whom God foreknew, He predestined to be conformed to the image of His son..."* - Romans 8:29

> *"God did not cast away His people whom He foreknew."* - Romans 11:2

Let's examine the last two Bible passages I cited. Yeshua is quoted as having said, *"God is spirit"* in John Chapter Four, so Spirit is the deity. These two verses from Romans together convey that a loving deity predestined everyone to become one with *The Spirit*. It's not that we are becoming "one;" but that we need to become *aware* that we already *are one* with the Spirit, our life-source. Becoming aware of our eternal nature as Spirit is what is meant by *"...to be conformed to the image of His son."* The word "son" implies that we are simply offspring of our divine source. One might ask, *"Did God, the Spirit, know me before I was born?"* The answer is a resounding, *"Yes!"* As mentioned, we are spirits within *The Spirit*, and we have existence because of that energy. Eternal separation can never be possible, except if we allow our mind to believe it were somehow so. To believe we are separate from our source is quite simply mistaken thinking due to not really knowing who we are. *If* we are already within the Eternal Being, Spirit, or God, then we *are* eternal, as well. This is what is meant by, *"...whom He foreknew."* We have always been *in Spirit;* therefore, we will always be and nothing can ever be lost. Something that has a beginning must have an end; for you cannot create the eternal from the temporal. I tell you the truth, *we have always been.* Those who would like to further explore this idea within the Bible can look to Psalm 139:16, which states:

> *"Your eyes have seen my unformed substance;*
> *And in your book were all written The days*
> *that were ordained for me, When as yet there*
> *was not one of them."*
> - Psalm 139:16 (NASB)

The *"unformed substance"* and *"the days that were ordained"* speak of our physical existence on the earthly plane. This is for a season, purpose, and quite temporary. Yet, we lived *before* we existed inside a suit of flesh that most believe to be who they are. Hell is produced in the mind that incorrectly identifies itself as being separated from its source (Spirit), believing the physical body to be the real person. But, we are not bodies of flesh; for we are spirits. Bodies are then a fading image animated by the inner person.

We are often instructed by Christians that *"God is everywhere. He is omnipresent."* If this is true, then God is indeed with us, *within* us, and thus would even be in Hell, if there were such a literal place. Honestly, if God is everywhere, even in Hell, then God would also have to be within people who were suffering in Hell! The Bible does indeed confirm the idea that God is with us no matter where we are, for David wrote:

> *"Where can I go from your Spirit? Where can I run from your presence? If I ascend into the skies, you are there; if I make my bed in the grave, behold, you are there."*
> - Psalm 139:7-8

Truly, if the Divine Spirit which many call *God* is omnipresent, then there cannot be any place such as Hell found anywhere outside of *The Spirit*. Nor can that change, for we are taught within Christianity that God himself never changes (Malachi 3:6). Still, many Christians are convinced that a holy God is separate from human beings. They see themselves, and the entire physical world, as being disconnected from Spirit. God, to them, is a puppet master who can pull strings, but there appears to be a Devil working hard at cutting the cords connecting us to our life-source. Believing illogical things, they wonder, *"How many people will God save?"* Heck, if God is all-powerful, would he ever lose one person to an inferior creature that some call the Devil? Furthermore, could any hurting human ever be beyond the help of such an almighty God? Christianity claims that God created this problem-causing Devil. If he did create such a bad egg, wouldn't it make sense that God could just as easily "crack" such a diabolical problem? Why would a good God ever create any evil entity that would vex him and his creation? Would God ever make such a mistake in judgment if he were *all-knowing*? No. Still, countless millions of Christians believe fearful nonsense, because they learn such things through listening to the ideas of fearful teachers using literal Bible interpretation. One would think by doing so, they might at least recognize a few of the obvious problems of believing in an eternal Hell, many of which I have pointed out. They somehow miss Yeshua's true message of our oneness with Divinity, sadly duping others into believing the same false teachings of a separate God and a fearful Hell. By teaching Hell is a real place, some Christians are successful at convincing people that they need saved from a possible destiny of eternal torment.

We read two important accounts of Yeshua, I wish to reference, in the New Testament. The first of which is when his disciples ask him, *"Who then shall be saved?"* Yeshua's reply was simply, *"The things that are impossible with men are possible with God."* He answered them quite plainly that *all* would be saved. When humans limit their reasoning, salvation of all seems impossible. But, mankind as a whole needs saved from such thinking, and all it requires is a change of mind. Many tend to think, *"Surely, some of the worst people we know have to suffer forever."* As humans, we base such ideas upon how poorly others have lived their lives while on Earth. But, to think that a vengeful god punishes the wicked forever is not how life works. God does not punish people; people punish themselves. Subconsciously, we create our own suffering and unwittingly implement our own punishment. We are creators, but unfortunately we do not comprehend just how powerful our ability

to create can be.  Remember, I mentioned when we
choose to harm others, we bring about emotional
suffering, a trial from and for ourselves.  Self-
condemnation is something that may appear as
judgment from a divine being, but is really our inner
conscience trying to help us to think differently.  We
beat ourselves up and find it impossible to forgive
our own shortcomings.  Suffering, such as this, can be
experienced by people on either side of the grave.
This *is* hell.  We should realize that hell is attainable
now and something we create with the power of the
mind.  Therefore, we choose how long we spend in
turmoil.  *This hell* is the bottomless pit that is easy to
fall into but hard to rise out of; and it is something
that much of Christianity is masterful at perpetuating.
Yeshua plainly stated *who* produces hell if we pay
close attention to the words I shared previously from
the Gospel of Matthew:

> *"What sorrow awaits you teachers of religious
> law and you Pharisees.  Hypocrites!  For you
> cross land and sea to make one convert, and
> then you turn that person into twice the child
> of hell you yourselves are!"*
> - Matthew 23:15 (NLT)

We read that Yeshua spoke these words to the Jewish,
religious leaders of his day, who were misleading
others into false beliefs.  The Greek word, translated
as *hell* in this passage, is actually *gehenna*, whose
meaning I previously noted as being a place of

idolatry and former trash dump outside of Jerusalem two thousand years ago. Knowing this, it is easy to understand this verse reveals that harmful religious ideas, used to lure converts to a religion, fill recruits' minds with rubbish and false idols they believe to be of God. Harmful religion, we learn, is to blame for much of the hell within many people's minds.

Allow me to compare one of the biblical passages I recently noted with another verse of interest:

> "...*the gates of hell shall not prevail...*"
> - Matthew 16:18 (KJV)

> "*(I) have the keys of hell and of death.*"
> - Revelation 1:18 (KJV) (a passage from a vision said to be of Yeshua speaking)

I love examining these two verses together; because if we believe Hell to be an eternal place of suffering where a good God imprisons evil people, then why would there be gates and keys? Keys have only one purpose and that is to unlock something. If these are the words of Yeshua, why would he bother declaring, "*I have the keys of hell and death,*" if they were not to be used? As I mentioned earlier, why would he also state, "*the gates of hell will not prevail,*" if hell were to hold captives forever? Let me remind the reader that a prison without gates is no longer a place capable of holding prisoners. Again, Yeshua must have taught hell as being a mental condition, meaning truth is the key to unlocking the prison of the mind that is lost.

Let's consider fear.  When the mind succumbs to fear, torment is suffered.  Fear ensnares a person, creating a very effective mental prison cell that, unfortunately, will not disappear until faced.  And, so it is also with the damaging Christian dogma of an eternal Hell, which boxes people into following religious rules in order to try and please an angry god in the hope that judgment may be avoided.  But, how can we run from our own self?  Can we ever avoid facing the things deep within us?  The fear created by allowing ourselves to succumb to nonsense establishes subtle control within a person.  It is not freeing but a form of sickness within the mind.

While writing this book, I contemplated how a simple fear of mine had controlled me, albeit subtly, for years.  So, I decided to embark on a quest to eliminate this small, personal hell of mine that was only occasionally torturing me.  You see, I have had a fear of thrill rides, such as roller coasters and especially those which cause one to experience sensations of falling.  I have ridden numerous roller coasters since the times of my adolescence, but still, I feel anxiety about going on any thrill ride which may pose a challenge to my inner fear.  So, I decided to challenge this fear while at a well-known amusement park.  I made it my personal mission to go on every big coaster and attraction my family could throw at me.  As I rode each thrill ride, I could see how my mind had previously produced fear that was unwarranted and made the experience worse within my head than the actual ride itself could be. I was silently chuckling to myself as I overcame these fears and felt freedom at last - or so I thought. As I was about to enter the line for one of the rides that had frightened me the most and the longest, I wanted to back out. I struggled badly within my own self torment, as my brain produced fear of major intensity. While I stood there at the entrance of the thrill ride, I eventually calmed my thoughts and deadened the fear, willingly choosing to walk in and face my terror. As I experienced my final amusement park ride, I allowed myself to relax and enjoy the moment, and in truth, it was thrilling. What was even more incredible was that I was able to shut down the part of my brain that wanted me to react to fear, allowing me to make a conscious decision to live in the moment and in peace. I no longer had to react to fear, for it was much better to identify it as being false and move beyond its stranglehold. Through this little experiment of mine, I was able to find enjoyment during the experiences which my head repeatedly told me I should fear. Instead of fear controlling us, we just need to learn to take control of fear.

My point is this: We can expose the false ideas of religion by simply identifying fear. If we choose to address the fearful things found within Christianity, we then allow ourselves to logically examine them. And, if we logically examine Christian teachings by not allowing fear to determine our beliefs, we will eventually realize that the teachings of a Hell, a Devil, and an angry God are illogical and quite false. When religious instructors choose to promote fear, such as fear of eternal punishment, fear of a vengeful God, or fear of a Devil and demons, they place people on an emotional roller coaster that is difficult to overcome unless faced. Many Christians will not face these fears, but somehow believe fearing an eternal Hell will bring peace. The reply from converts to such Christian ideas will simply say, "You are wrong. I no longer fear Hell, for I am saved. I haven't felt this peaceful in all my life." I want to say to them, "Oh, fool! You have no idea, for you have not explored the depths of your beliefs!" But, to do so will not cause them to hear the truth. The power of their mind has shut itself down from considering anything else possibly being true. Unfortunately, those with closed minds will often require a traumatic experience to shake them awake. It will be at that point of crisis that they will consider their choices have been incorrect. This is unfortunate, but many Christians are not looking and listening deep enough. If they did, they would know that they simply buried their fears down deep. They are unable to comprehend that they were at one time in peace, until another told them they shouldn't be. Someone told them they were less than whole, broken, and in need of escape from their wretched condition. Thus, the hell that was created in their mind did not exist until some religious snake whispered the idea to them, much like the story of Eve in Eden.  I am sure people who tell others they need to be saved from Hell have good intentions, but what they create is difficult emotional trauma for people.  They do so by projecting their own fears upon the other person.  The convert wrongly perceives the new found fear within them as being "conviction from God."  Their conversion to the false is then complete.  This hellish idea is planted in the mind of the person when they are weakened to believing a lie about themselves.  Little do they know that hell is never outside of a person, nor is it a place.  Hell can only be found within a fearing mind.

I understand the traditional teaching of hell better than most, as I previously shared how I went on a journey to find out the truth about God, death and Hell.  My thoughts about such ideas plagued me for many years.  Unfortunately, there was a time when I became a teacher of such false doctrines and trapped others in my fears about being tormented forever.  Back then, I was unable to comprehend how much damage I was causing people, including myself.  I thought I was saving the world!  Now, I feel compelled to rescue people from the same Christian instruction that damaged me and consequently others who listened to the garbage I had told them about a wrathful God who forever punishes the wicked.  Fears are something we should dispel, not advance in others.

As I contemplate my own experiences with fearful

things, it brings to mind how I have overcome other fears in my life. This may sound silly, but there was a time when I would never wear shorts or take my shirt off, for example. Looking back, I now understand that it was because I feared that others would make fun of my physical body. As a kid, I was teased by someone for my flesh having not seen the light of day for a long time. That teasing caused me to never want to experience ridicule again, so I hid what I perceived to be my unsightly parts underneath the shield of clothing. Of course, this made it so I never wanted to wear shorts, or ever go swimming, which was also a former fear of mine. I eventually overcame my fear of water by taking swimming lessons as an adolescent. It was a struggle for me, but over time, I soon learned to swim. With each victory in the pool, the stronger I felt, and the smaller my fears became. Now, I look at many of my former fears and realize that I fueled most of them by believing my body was *the real me*.

I wonder how many fears each of us have that cause us not to live life to the fullest. Thinking back, I remember being afraid of many things during my youth, especially dogs. When I was about eight years old, I ran from two Boxers that gave chase to me. One of them bit me during the end of their pursuit. Over time, this crippled me mentally to the point of sheer torment whenever I would come in contact with larger dogs that could possibly pose a threat. Just the bark of a dog would startle my mind greatly. By the time I was a teenager, the fear was still with me. One

day while walking down a sidewalk, a German
Shepherd came barreling down a driveway and was
determined to attack me. Instead of following my
fear that said, *"Run,"* I decided to stare the dog down
and yell at it. And, so I did. The German Shepherd
immediately put the brakes on and slowly proceeded
forward, but I could now see fear in his eyes as we
stared each other down, both determined not to let
the other win. Finally, the dog's owner came out of
the house, called the dog off, and I continued my
walk down the street with my fear of being bitten by
dogs removed.

Why should we miss living today by continuing to
fear a doubtful future? Facing our fears is the only
way to make them go away. When we feel fear, the
fear itself will either be intensified by giving it power,
or reduced and possibly eliminated by refusing to
believe it warrants any merit. Accepting fear, by
reacting to it, is validation to the mind that a threat is
real. There is great personal freedom in knowing that
I am in control and so is everyone of their own mind.
This has motivated me to explore the fears I am able
to identify as existing in my life. The intent of such
self-exploration is to expose what is false, and in the
process, find freedom that brings real peace. This is
why understanding fear is important if one is to
escape the teaching of an eternal Hell. As I have
explained before, hell is the mind that believes false
things to be true. The past takes hold of the person
through fear and refuses to allow one to live in the

now, as it always poses the "*What if...?*"
question. "*What if you are stung by a bee when looking at
the flowers?*" "*What if someone makes fun of your
appearance if you wear the blue shoes?*" and so forth.
Through this method of madness, the ego will play a
shell game of control through fear by bringing to
remembrance one's past experience, and thus cause
the person to wrestle with an uncertain future. This
way, the mind is not allowed to have peace in the
present, even though today is all that exists. The
moment is lost and fear increased, for the past and
future only exist in the mind's memory. Yes, ideas
concerning our future are formed in our minds from
past experiences we have remembered. This is how
the *visible me* operates, by animating the false into a
painful way of existence. Thankfully, we have the
ability to step back and identify that our past and
future are illusionary, for they are not reality. Only,
*now* is real.

Being captive to our past is what death and hell are:
the condition of being mentally separated from our
reality. It bears repeating that *The Fall* (being
spiritually dead) is best symbolized in the *Garden of
Eden* story, when Adam and Eve believe that God, the
Spirit, is somehow separated from them. Those who
are unaware of the Spirit within, their true self, are
indeed "dead" to the knowledge they are an extension
of the life-giving force. They subsist completely
unaware of their oneness with Spirit. Hell and death
are, therefore, creations of the mind that are misled

and in need of truth:

> *"And a poor man named Lazarus was laid at his
> gate, covered with sores, and longing to be fed with
> the crumbs which were falling from the rich man's
> table; besides, even the dogs were coming and
> licking his sores. Now the poor man died and was
> carried away by the angels to Abraham's bosom;
> and the rich man also died and was buried. In
> Hades he lifted up his eyes, being in torment, and
> saw Abraham far away and Lazarus in his bosom.
> And he cried out and said, 'Father Abraham, have
> mercy on me, and send Lazarus so that he may dip
> the tip of his finger in water and cool off my tongue,
> for I am in agony in this flame.' But Abraham said,
> 'Child, remember that during your life you received
> your good things, and likewise Lazarus bad things;
> but now he is being comforted here, and you are in
> agony. And besides all this, between us and you
> there is a great chasm fixed, so that those who wish
> to come over from here to you will not be able, and
> that none may cross over from there to us.'"*
> - Luke 16:20-26 (NASB)

Because hell is the state of the human mind believing
it is fearfully separate from the Divine; it is therefore
lost and unable to communicate with Spirit. The
Spirit is always speaking, but the mind that is focused
on the exterior world is unaware, being unable to
hear the inner voice. Regarding the prior parable of
*Lazarus and the Rich Man*, many Christians believe this

is a literal portrait of Hell and not a spiritual riddle. But, this is indeed a parable. We know this, because attempting to understand it literally does not make sense. For example, if we could see others we care about suffering in Hell, as in this story, would anyone ever be at peace? I am sure Lazarus would have wanted to help the rich man but was unable to do so. Why, not? The simple spiritual lesson is this: we have the ability to create this gulf *within* us by believing things that are contrary to truth. In other words, this is the story of what happens to a person who denies the Spirit within, caring only for the things of the physical world. A division is created within the person, and two people are at odds: the rich man and the poor man. The rich man only cares about the things of the external world, while the poor man, represented by Lazarus in the story, is denied a place. If we choose to believe we are the rich man, we will look outside our self for aid, but that will not yield help, for only we are the creator of our condition. The rich man is the visible me, the false you who lives life sumptuously, only caring about physical pleasures. The earthly world helped us to create this ego-driven way of thinking. But, Lazarus is our spirit man, the real you, who is starved and begging to be allowed to have a place. He sits at the gates being locked out, the same gates of hell that Yeshua stated would not prevail. The parable reveals there are two people within us. In this story, we learn of the effects of a split mind, a hellish condition we should realize as being mental suffering. Who do we choose to identify as being the real me?  Are you Spirit, one with your Divine source?  Or, are you simply a person stumbling through the world, unaware of who you are?  The rich man can only see himself as being somehow separate and isolated from others and from God...Spirit.  If we choose to believe this lie to be true, our peace, our fellow man, and even God appear severed away from us.  So, it is indeed possible that what people choose to believe in their heart will become quite true to them.  The rich man lives life outwardly and by doing so, falsely forges his own prison by the power of his mis-creating intellect.  The fear by which he lives his earthly life eventually becomes a horrible nightmare, an illusion of self-suffering that he never could have imagined he would create for himself.  Physical death does not heal a split mind or end emotional suffering, and so the illusion of separation will remain even on the other side of the grave.  Healing can still come but only by changing incorrect thinking.  It is time to ask ourselves, "*Do I have division within me?  And if so, will I seek to have the false reconciled by allowing the spirit man, that exists within, to have a place?*"

The Spirit's place is that of a wise voice that ever guides us toward freedom from our fear.  To many Christians, fear *appears* as being truth; but when truth shines like a light into darkness (our misunderstanding), then the false ceases to exist (for it is revealed to be illusion).  When truth is understood, fearful creations, such as hell, will disappear and no longer have power over the mind that had previously fallen victim to believing the false. Knowing truth makes it impossible to once again fall victim to frightening inventions of the mind.

In understanding fear, I suggest we define it as, "*a false perception that produces confusion, demanding a reaction that silences the voice of Spirit.*" Understanding this idea is the beginning of locating our source of truth, while learning to identify the forms of fear that are false. Fear can sometimes easily fool the mind. Some might think while reading this that fear can be good. For example one might say, "*It is good to fear being run over by a train, for I will be more cautious when near train tracks.*" To me, this example of train tracks, and the fear they might cause, can be understood differently. "*If I do not yet want to experience death of the physical body, it would be a good idea to be aware of the possibility of an oncoming train while crossing train tracks.*" At least this way I am not identifying the body as being who I am, but only as something I choose to use as a vehicle to operate within the physical world. Fear is produced by all our brains, but it is what we do with the fear that is most important. Am I believing fear when it tells me that my body is who I really am, or am I seeing fear for what it is and not choosing to be controlled by it? We should learn to identify fear when we experience it, and then choose to calm our mind and make rational decisions from a higher perspective, remaining unmotivated by the panic we feel. This way we can train ourselves from being reactionary.

By permitting ourselves to be subject to the world outside of us, we allow ourselves no other choice but to become reactionary. The amygdala found within each person's brain creates chemicals which produce fear known as the "*fight or flight*" response. It is most basic in nature and is used by the animal kingdom, being quite necessary for their physical survival. If a rabbit sees a predator, for example, it will often choose to flee using the "flight response." If, say a wolf is cornered by a man, the animal will likely choose to fight in order to survive. This is the "fight response." Our brain similarly creates a beastly response to the external environment, which pushes us to want to react by either fighting or running away from the perceived threat. If we, as human beings, wish to transcend and move beyond such basic of animal responses, then we need to see fear for what it is. We can do so by recognizing frightening motivators, choosing not to react, thus at least allowing ourselves time to reason. Let us learn to label fears as being false, so we do not allow them to dissuade us from following our inner guide. The ultimate goal is to allow Spirit to have a voice in our decisions. This is to allow the true, inner person to live.

In Matthew 8:26, we read Yeshua stated, "*Why are you so fearful, O' you of little faith?*" The Greek word translated in this quote as "faith" better means "confidence." This passage clearly shows that fear robs us of confidence when allowed to have a place within us. For all of us, how we perceive ourselves determines how we act, or more likely *react* to life around us. If we truly do not know who we are, then false perceptions will cause us to believe lies, things contrary to the truth of the *real you*. For these reasons, we need to understand that people's perceptions, understandings, and expectations in life will vary according to who they believe they are and what they allow to motivate them. I should note that "belief" is a form of doubt, and really just an extension of hope. I mentioned in a previous chapter that hope is a form of fear. So, *belief* is a creation of fear, though belief (as well as hope) *can* at least be a step in the right direction toward knowing truth (which is better than having no belief, which means no direction at all). Many Christians are taught they should have faith (which is belief); but there is a distinct difference between believing something and knowing something. It is better to know something is true, rather than believing, or hoping it is.

Let's explore belief, hope, and faith a bit further. *To believe* in something is to say one is unsure, and positive belief can be equated with "having faith." Faith in the positive is produced by hope. In the New Testament, this idea is touched upon by the writer of Hebrews:

> "*Now, faith is the substance of things hoped for...*"

- Hebrews 11:1 (KJV)

We often *believe* things, because we hope they are
true; but we also sometimes believe things because
we hope the opposite is true.  This is because we
simply do not know what the truth is, but as people,
we typically choose to hope for the best.

*To know* something, means one has grasped the truth.
There is nothing contrary to it, for truth is
unchanging, immovable, and thus, eternal.  Knowing
truth is life-changing and obviously, much greater
than belief, hope or faith; for one can no longer
believe in things false that were once temporarily
believed to be true.  Believing positive things can
indeed be good, in the sense that it may lead one
toward the direction of eventually knowing truth.
However, hope, faith and belief are still forms of fear,
caused by lack of knowledge.  We fear due to our
beliefs in what we do not understand, and thus hope
for the best.  But, believing and hoping are not the
same as knowing, and there is a distinct difference:
knowing truth removes fear.

If we try to understand truth from the perspective of
looking externally at this temporary, physical world,
it will prove too difficult to comprehend.  The reason
for this is because everything we experience
externally with our physical body is passing away
and is, therefore, not truth which is eternal.  The
physical environment we navigate within has created

a limited perspective, from which we are unable to see the entire picture of who we are in the world or our role within it. And so, truth must be comprehended from within one's being, the heart of mankind which is the eternal Spirit. There is no other source for truth or any other way to receive the higher knowledge one might desire.

Knowing the truth of who we are brings peace and freedom. We are eternal Spirit. Yeshua is quoted as having said:

> *"and you will know the truth, and the truth will make you free."* - John 8:32 (NASB)

If we turn this passage around, we could say it this way, *"The truth we know will make us free."* Knowing truth is the magical pill that frees the mind from a state of hell. If we do not know that we are eternal Spirit, then we will always identify with things that appear true but are false. Fear creates all false things that we believe to be real. This is especially so when one does not understand, and chooses to believe, the *visible me* as being who they are. We need to be true to ourselves. That is done by looking within and recognizing fear when it is the motivator behind the things we choose to do, or not do. Fear suffocates people, causing them to: lack self-confidence, fret over what people think of them, feel defeated, attack others, become angry, feel anxious, be intimidated, want to hide, suffer depression, worry, be concerned, doubt, become apathetic, lack self-control, fear failure, fear loss, fear suffering, fear the unknown, fear people, feel guilty, suffer under self-condemnation, have low self-esteem, and, of course, fear a vengeful God. Perhaps by these examples, you may be able to understand how debilitating fear can be to a person and just how much it rules our lives. How many of us walking the Earth are motivated in some form or fashion by fear within us? I would venture to say that most people are driven in directions they were not meant to go by fear and thus, have missed who they really are as people. Hell is the result of such thinking.

Permit me to recap some important points concerning fear, the energy that creates inner hell. I suggested recognizing forms of fear as being important. When we recognize them, we should work removing them. We fear what we do not understand, so seek knowledge. Fear is learned, so let's change our thinking. Fear is attached to our past, affecting our future, and can be likened to a skilled illusionist working diligently to keep us from living in the present. Know that everyone has the power to overcome fearful thinking. The truth we understand removes fear and empowers us to victory over all that may come our way. Our fear keeps us from being who we are, so fear is a doorway to run through. See a door? Run through it! Remember that fear is created by us (and not God), so *we can* control how we choose to observe life, rather than being unnerved by terrifying images the mind produces. When fears are faced, they eventually vanish. The more fear is confronted, the more powerless it becomes until it no longer exists. Face your doubts, your worries, your fears, for peace and understanding will then replace them.

You should now understand why hell, truly a state of suffering produced by fear, is already being experienced by most through incorrect personal identification with the ego, the false person, the *visible me*. Hell is not a place of eternal punishment, as much of Christianity teaches, but the condition of a fearful mind. Certainly, if we consider such a manner of thinking and how it affects us, we can comprehend how suffering occurs. It is fair to say that a person who does not know who they are, is a lost soul. A day comes for each person when we must know who we are, or risk distress. The worst hell imaginable is a mental state of confusion and inner turmoil found within a person who is suffering, not knowing where to turn. All of life's failures and mistakes may seem to weigh heavily upon such a soul, appearing as though an angry God were bringing guilt and condemnation upon their shoulders. Darkness from misunderstanding can cloud the mind with a great burden that is most difficult to bear. Know that every person can be awakened from such a nightmare in their season. Even when things appear darkest, it is never too late for anyone to embark down the path of self-discovery, which is the only way to personal freedom. It's a small, less traveled path to the place where the true self is found, but it is the only road to forgiveness, healing, peace and joy. Love ultimately frees all, vanquishing every form of fear - hell.

# 5 Demons, Devils & Satan

If true hell is a correctable mental condition, then the
Christian belief in hellish creatures must also be the
creation of a mistaken mind that has succumbed
to fear. We'll explore this idea, but allow me to first
explain that most of Christianity believes demons and
the Devil are evil entities responsible for wreaking
havoc upon mankind. Christians are traditionally
taught that Satan (another name used for the Devil)
and his minions preside over Hell. The goal of this
dark force, we learn, is to first lure as many people as
possible into committing sin. By doing so, Hell is
enlarged with masses of unfit humans; hence the plan
of God's creation is partially destroyed for eternity.
We are left to conclude that an all-powerful, all-
knowing God is not only responsible for generating
evil but also remains powerless to stop such a train
wreck until it has permanently psychologically
damaged a significant portion of mankind. If God is
omnipresent (present everywhere), as Christianity
proclaims, God must also be in Hell with such
malevolent devils. For if we believe Hell is a place,
and God's presence cannot be contained, then surely
such an omnipresent deity must be in the infernal
regions, too. Hell, however, is not a place of eternal
punishment, but instead a correctable state of mind.
Should we find ourselves mentally suffering in hell,
know that the divine Spirit indeed is ever-present to
guide us home.

The creatures that can inhabit and torment a mind are nothing more than products of an incorrect thought process. Minds that have strayed, through faulty beliefs based upon our own mistaken identity crisis (not knowing who we are), produce fearful ideas. Such thinking can cause a person to believe the worst exists somewhere outside of them, never comprehending that we are the creators of our own monsters. Then demons and the Devil become real, contrary to the belief that surely we would never purposely harm ourselves. We have our best interest in mind. We think that the Devil must have made me do it, or maybe Satan did it to me. Do you wish to believe our lives are really subject to external, evil forces that lie in wait? Perhaps in your search to locate demons, you forgot to look in the most obvious hiding spot. What if the Devil and demons that we fear are found hidden within all of us? Wouldn't that be the worst fate? Not really, for if we can identify that which bewitches us, we can then choose to not be subject to further suffering.

The Bible uses much symbolism, especially with the use of a Devil and demons within its pages. Such imagery is used to convey ideas that are not to be interpreted as literal representations. Allow me to specify that our own misguided thoughts *are* the biblical demons that plague our minds. Have you ever heard it said that someone who is struggling with emotional issues battles demons? The demons we choose to battle are the false thoughts we elect to manufacture. We can easily, but quite mistakenly, create beliefs that are false, unwittingly giving life to them. Knowing that we are responsible for creating wrong beliefs, I choose to call such thoughts "creatures." Creatures can be harmful thoughts that haunt the minds of those who allow them to exist. The unsound mind that creates and believes false ideas is represented in the Bible as being "the Devil," or "Satan." It is taught within Christianity that Satan, the supreme Devil, rules over all demons. This idea, in a figurative sense, is true. The name Satan simply means "*adversary*," and when we allow ourselves to believe things about ourselves that are false, we become our own worst enemy. It is this adversary (*the visible me*) that can be defeated by simply choosing not to believe in its false, fearful creations.

We should consider mistakes in our thinking as merely temporary obstacles that divert us from knowing the truth about ourselves. A state of mind suffering hell is manifested by a person who is bound by false beliefs they have chosen to accept as being real. Such a one lives in periods of torment created by their own mind, which vibrantly produces frightening images and sounds. The mind is able to project illusions that seem to be authentic, real experiences. Accordingly, many Christians choose to believe in demons and devils, because their one-time pure mind was unfortunately contaminated by someone else's idea that they should be concerned about terrific, unseen forces. The mind is a powerful, creative force that if allowed to run wild, can bring one unnecessary suffering. It seems a substantial amount of people unintentionally bring all sorts of injury to themselves. Let this be your guide to knowing what is false and what is true: we unknowingly choose suffering when we select fearful things over truth. Like the teaching of an eternal Hell, Christian ideas of a Devil and demons are fearful and therefore must be false. Allow me to attempt to bring understanding concerning such frightening entities by explaining their more relevant, spiritual meaning, as well as their origins within Christianity.

Christian stories suggesting the existence of an evil Devil is nothing more than a fairy tale. In the 1939 movie, *The Wizard of Oz*, we learn that everyone is afraid of a wizard until a young girl confronts him and reveals him to be just an old man pulling strings behind a curtain. Likewise, Christianity chooses to use a veil of fear, but there be very few who are willing to expose the lie by peering behind the dogma, in order to learn the truth. Frightening images are intentionally used to keep converts from peering behind Christianity's curtain. But, what is there to lose? What if we choose to investigate the reasons behind why we believe fearful things and discover that only freeing, more peaceful answers await us? Wouldn't it be grand to no longer be a slave to fear?

Unfortunately, many are deeply enslaved to fear

through religious instruction, yet Yeshua (you may call him Jesus), stood opposed to such ideas. Fearful religious teachings strengthen untruths, causing us to ignore the inner voice. Freedom from such indoctrination is most difficult. Typified in Matthew four, we read Jesus is tempted by a devil, his own mind-empowered ego, seeking to gain and maintain control of him through fear:

> *"Then Jesus was led by the Spirit into the wilderness to be enticed by the Devil."* - Matthew 4:1

The word translated in this verse as *Devil*, is the Greek word *diabolos*. In other places within the New Testament, it is translated as *Satan*. The word itself means *"false accuser; slanderer,"* but is wrongly interpreted as being some evil entity that pursues Jesus in the desert. This passage found in Matthew is better understood as teaching us about ourselves. The wilderness is a word used to describe the mind of mankind, often a lonesome wasteland...barren due to lack of spiritual understanding. Drought within the mind is caused by lack of water, and water is frequently used symbolically in the Bible to represent Spirit. Yeshua, we read, was led by the Divine Spirit to face his wilderness, which I earlier alluded to as really being a confrontation with the ego, the *visible me*. This Devil that controls the collective mind of mankind seeks to sustain its own existence, and thus points to things outside of us in order to lead us away from the Spirit within. The rest of the passage I have taken the liberty to interpret a bit differently:

> "*The tempter came to him and said, 'If you are the Son of Spirit, tell these stones to become bread.'*
>
> *Yeshua answered, 'It is written: Man does not exist on bread alone, but on every word that comes from the mouth of the Spirit.'*
>
> *Then the Ego took him to the holy city and had him stand on the highest point of the temple. 'If you are the Son of Spirit,' he said, 'cast yourself down. For it is written:*
>
> *He will command his messengers concerning you, and they will lift you up in their hands, so that you will not strike your foot against a stone.'*
>
> *Yeshua answered him, 'It is also written: Do not put the Supreme Spirit to the test.'*
>
> *Again, the Ego took him to a very high mountain and showed him all the kingdoms of the world and their splendor. 'I will give you all of this,' he said, 'if you will lower yourself by paying attention to me.'*
>
> *Yeshua said to him, 'Away from me, Accuser! For it is written: Pay attention to the Supreme Spirit,*

*and serve him only.'*

*Then the Ego left him alone, and messengers came and attended him."* - Matthew 4:2-11

There is much to point out in this passage that reveals the battle waging within us, between our mind-created ego, and the true spirit person we are. Notice that the ego tries to entice Yeshua away from following Spirit by focusing on three things (all found outside of him):

1) Reliance upon the physical world. Yeshua chooses not to allow the physical world to become his source for truth.

2) Mortality. Yeshua faces fear concerning his own death, a true battle over whether or not we know the truth concerning our own immortality.

3) Material gain. Yeshua sought not to be temporarily satisfied by inevitably worthless, material riches, such as power, popularity or wealth.

When the ego, or *visible me*, was no longer allowed to direct Yeshua's life, then the Spirit became his sole guide. The passage further declares that messengers in Spirit (sometimes translated *angels*), attended to him. Angels often represent higher thoughts, messages of truth from Spirit that are wonderfully healing. I should further clarify that when we choose to look within ourselves and listen to the voice of Spirit, we will often receive direction from benevolent spirit messengers. Enlightened spirits within Spirit help us to understand who we are, granting us assistance in gaining our freedom. This entire passage in Matthew is a parable that reveals who we are, and the struggle taking place within us. It informs us that when we decide to change our own mode of operating, we too can experience spirituality. Spirituality is knowing we are eternal Spirit and choosing to live a life in-tune with the inner voice.

When we recognize that parables within the Bible should be interpreted figuratively, such as the example found in Matthew Chapter Four, light shines into our mind and peace is the result. It is then that we begin to comprehend why we must identify and face our fears in order to expose their source. When the fearful teachings of Christianity are weakened, it enables us to reduce the false chatter of the ego, allowing us to better discern the real you, the voice of Spirit within. My explanation of the parable, in Matthew Chapter Four, may have left you wondering, *"Why did Jesus say several times, 'It is written?'"* Yeshua used scriptures to eliminate his own religious fears; for what better way is there to find freedom from fearful ideas than to cite the fallacies found within their source in order to dispel them? This way, he was able to first eliminate religion within himself, before speaking even more boldly against it publicly.

Finding liberty from the shackles of legalistic
Judaism, Yeshua then sought to help others gain their
freedom, too. He did so by speaking directly against
the corrupt, religious institution of his day. Any
religious organization that promotes fear can be
symbolically equated to being a dragon as found in
the last chapter of the Bible:

> "*...the great dragon was cast out, that old serpent
> called the Devil, and Satan, which deceiveth the
> whole world...*" - Revelation 12:9 (KJV)

Knowing you are now aware that the egocentric mind
of man is described as being a devil or Satan in the
Bible, it should be easy to see that man's collective
ego-driven thinking can also be equated with a
dragon. A dragon is the perfect example to represent
mankind's ego, for it is largely troublesome, fearful
and difficult to slay. The dragon depicts the debased
mind-set of humanity as a whole, something that
needs healed. Religion, then, is simply a physical
manifestation of this collective ego. We could call it
an outward indication of an inward issue. Therefore,
a dragon can also symbolically represent a man-
made, ego-driven, religious system, as Revelation 12:9
may suggest. Non-spiritual leaders of such religious
institutions are motivated by the ego, fitting to be
called what leads them: devils.

The Bible seems to have an affinity towards using
reptiles, like dragons and snakes, as symbols to

illustrate negative thinking. Because religion, like Christianity, can deceive people by causing them to lose sense of their true person, Yeshua preferred to call the leaders of such institutions snakes and vipers:

> *"You snakes! You brood of vipers! How will you escape being condemned to hell?"* - Matthew 23:33 (NIV)

As I shared previously, in Genesis we read the account of a serpent causing mankind (symbolized by Adam and Eve) to believe things contrary to the truth of who we really are. Genesis means *the beginning*, so from the beginning mankind was deluded by believing falsehoods. Knowing this, Yeshua chose to appropriately label ego-inspired religious leaders as being snakes, for they were misdirecting people away from their true identity through the guise of religion. The ego, or *visible me*, is indeed the viper that whispers doubts within our minds. Similarly, religious leaders who lead others astray can be equated with being such external representations of ego.

Christian leaders and teachers who poison people, being lost themselves, should rightly be called vipers. They deceive followers through playing to emotions, wrongly feeding the egotistical, carnal thought process of man which is only able to survive through identification with the outside world. By doing so, they distract people from finding the true person; all-the-while creating converts who wrongly exist with a split mind:

> *"A double minded man is unstable in all his ways."* - James 1:8 (KJV)

Such Christian evangelists often make people powerless, like wounded beasts relying on someone or something else to sustain them. Though they do not understand it, proponents of Christianity often speak of a *beast nature*, or *carnal nature*, knowing it is in opposition to the Spirit. Christianity teaches that the beast nature is who we really are, but this is not true. The beast nature is the false you, the ego; the *visible me*. The ego-way of thinking operates opposite the Spirit, from the outside environment inward, instead of the Spirit within being allowed to provide sustenance. This change in direction away from one's center is really a disregard for a person's inner compass. Almost the whole of Christianity does not steer a person to look within for answers, because they teach that man is intrinsically bad. By doing so, they tell people the source for good cannot be found within. They oppose being single-minded (which *is* Christ), unknowingly becoming anti-Christ as a result of trying to silence the guiding voice of Spirit. By not acknowledging its existence, navigation through life can soon become chaotic. Always remember that to ignore the Spirit is to silence the voice of the Divine within one's being.

When the *visible me*, the man of sin (or mis-thinking), has become self-apparent, we have the responsibility to choose a different direction. The Spirit within reveals this false identity that each of us have given power to in our lives. In a sense, because we allow the *visible me* to rule, it has become a god that has temporarily replaced the Divine within us. Similarly, Paul wrote about a man of destruction that operates as a god, being revealed (to us) and sitting in the temple:

> "*Don't let anyone deceive you in any way, for (that day will not come) until the rebellion occurs and the man of lawlessness is revealed, the man doomed to destruction. He will oppose and will exalt himself over everything that is called God or is worshiped, so that he sets himself up in God's temple, proclaiming himself to be God.*" - II Thessalonians 2:3-4 (NIV)

Most Christians are looking for the Devil, or even an Antichrist to surface somewhere outside of themselves, failing to recognize that a form of anti-Christ is already at work within them. The word "Christ" means *anointing*. When we forsake the Divine Spirit within us, by turning away from our center of being, we not only lie to ourselves but fail to recognize the *anointing of Spirit* as God. Consequently, when we allow the *visible me* to be in power within our mind, the temple - the person, is for a time corrupted within as the Spirit is not allowed to reign from the throne of our hearts. This is perhaps why Paul said:

> *"Don't you know that you yourselves are God's temple and that God's Spirit lives in you?"* - I Corinthians 3:16 (NIV)

Yes, we can say we are the place where the Divine Spirit dwells, and not in some church building made by human hands. We do not need to go far to find God, for God is within us. When people look outside of themselves for God, the world becomes even more disconnected. With this type of thinking, the Almighty becomes distant and seemingly difficult to contact, as the deity is separate. God thus becomes our very distant hope who we rely upon, essentially making ourselves powerless even though the Divine rests within us. In an imagined world such as this, the mind further creates what would appear to be the exact opposite of a good God; an evil Devil and his minions who are out to get everyone (by the way, isn't it interesting that "evil" backwards, spells "live?"). For the mind that is delusional believes that unseen evil forces are the cause of all things deemed bad. And surely the Devil is responsible for all things wrong, as God would never be against us. And in truth, God isn't against anyone. When we believe in such duality, in such opposites, in such falsehoods, we empower the things that do not exist, effectively giving them life in our minds. These creations appear to be so real, yet they are false and only a hallucination. Should we take a moment to logically consider the belief in a literal devil, we may be able to realize this idea does not make sense. If there is an all-powerful God who is everywhere, then how could he allow such evil to somehow evade his presence in order to attack and persecute mankind? If a god outside of us thought it good that we overcome such an awful entity as the Devil or Satan, who would be more evil? Would it be the Devil, or the God who made such a Lord of Darkness? If God willingly created the Devil knowing he would inevitably do such horrible things to humanity (for God is all-knowing, Christianity tells us), then the Almighty would have to be more evil than the one whom he created. Could we ever trust in such a wicked deity, as Christianity would like us to do, to decide our fate? An unreliable God could never be relied upon.

Many Christians choose to believe in the Devil, whom they call Satan (or Lucifer), but to do so is to put one's faith and creative power toward producing the negative. I choose to do no such thing. Most denominations within Christianity, however, elect to teach that Satan was formerly an archangel who rebelled against God, eventually being banished from Heaven. In rebellion, the Devil then lured a third of the angels away from God, who we are taught have now become demons. This militia of demons is supposed to be evil agents of the Devil who are out to get all of mankind. Like the doctrine of an eternal Hell, the tale of demons and a Devil was purposely initiated by Roman Catholicism over a period of time but later was furthered by other denominations and sects within most of Christianity.

We should investigate the origin of the word "demon." *Demon* is Middle English, derived from the late Latin word *daemon*, which originated from the Greek word *daimon*. *Daimones* or *daimonion* are the plural forms of the word *daimon*. It is important to know this, because mis-translations of these Greek words in the New Testament of the Bible, are sometimes rendered as either *"demon"* or *"demons"* (and sometimes *devil* and *devils*). Furthermore, *daimonimozai* has been translated into the English language as *"demonized"* or *"demon-possessed."* There is a problem with all of these aforementioned translations: *daimons* were never demons, or even devils for that matter. Could the interpretation of these words have been changed by Bible translators in order to mean something different than what was originally intended by the Greek authors of the manuscripts contained within the New Testament? To find out, we must first look at what *daimones* actually were to the Greeks.

Though I already explained that the teachings of Devils and demons are best understood as being biblical parables of something false we create within us, there is still an additional understanding that I need to share regarding their origin. The belief in *daimones* can be traced back to ancient

Mesopotamia and the Babylonian culture, which organized such spirits into hierarchies and armies, much like guardian angels. So, it is not much of a surprise then, that in ancient Greek culture, *daimones* represented "divine beings." *Daimones* have been known by many different names (such as genii, and satyr), and were considered spirits of nature, cities, places, planets, stars and the like, having interaction in the affairs of humanity. They were believed to be god-like, ministering spirits, protective spirits, and at times, even the souls of the dead. Interestingly, like the souls or spirits of dead people, *daimones* were also recognized for having a nature capable of both good and bad. Predating Yeshua, and thus the New Testament, the ancient Greeks' belief in *daimones* appeared in the literature of many philosophers, including Homer, Socrates and Plato. Plato distinguished *daimones* as being middle-ranking creatures of the air, interacting between gods and mankind. Socrates not only described *daimones* as guardian spirits that everyone has around them, but also as the inner-voice that guided him in choosing to do right, rather than wrong. The Greeks believed *daimones* could haunt locations, guard property, possess human bodies, and even cause human sicknesses. Yet, they also believed that *daimones* were at times the spirits of the dead (ghosts) who could be sought for advice; and that *daimones* could also be messengers similar to modern beliefs in angels.

To the Greeks, the word *daimon* was often used for the

word "god" or "goddess," especially before the
Hellenistic period. But the word *daimon* could also
mean "the gods," "divine power, "fate," or "fortune,"
as well as a "spirit being." The adjective, *daimonios*,
often meant "inspired by heaven," "divine," "of
heaven," "by divine power," etc. The *Harper's
Dictionary of Classical Antiquities* (1897) has this to say
about the word *daemon* (the Latinized spelling
for *daimon*):

> "*Originally a term applied to deity in general,
> manifested in its active relation to human life,
> without special reference to any single divine
> personality. But as early Hesiod, the daemones
> appear as subordinates or servants of the higher
> gods. He gives the name especially to the spirits of
> the past age of gold, who are appointed to watch
> over men and guard them. In later times, too, the
> daemones were regarded as beings intermediate
> between the gods and mankind, forming, as it were,
> the retinue of the gods, representing their powers in
> activity, and intrusted with the fulfilment of their
> various functions. This was the relation, to take an
> instance, which the Satyrs and Sileni bore to
> Dionysus. But the popular belief varied in regard
> to these deities.*"

Perhaps the Greek idea of *daimones* could be more
easily summed up as being spirit entities,
encompassing those of a positive or negative
behavior. The widespread belief in *daimones* was

attacked over time by Christian church leaders in order to discredit these ancient Greek ideas. By the early 5th century, St. Augustine devoted two chapters of his book "*The City of God*" in pursuit of attacking pagan beliefs in *daimones*. Because people still believed in them, *daimones* purposely evolved into becoming "demons" (or devils) through the aid of Christian proponents. Then, church leaders simply defined demons as something evil. Demons were further taught by the leaders of Christianity as being the messengers and followers of the solitary leader of evil - Satan (Lucifer, the Devil). To create fear in people, the role of demons and the Devil were also embellished over time by Christianity. For example, St. Thomas Aquinas perpetuated beliefs in the demonic by claiming demons are sometimes permitted to punish mankind, being sent by God. He also taught that what may appear to be miraculous, such as natural disasters and bad weather, can be caused by the power of Satan and demons. Through such tactics, Christian leaders over centuries were able to unjustly convince people that *daimones* were nothing more than evil demons, something to be feared.

To further my point that Christianity took liberties with translations of the Greek *daimones* (as well as its various forms) in order to support church doctrines, allow me to share a perfect example of the Greek language being twisted within the Bible. In the books of Acts and I Corinthians, we might notice the same word *daimonion* translated as both "gods" and "demons," but in truth the translation from the original Greek language is better read as "gods" in both passages, due to the context in which the Apostle Paul was using *daimonion* in his argument against idol worship:

> "*A group of Epicurean and Stoic philosophers began to dispute with him. Some of them asked, 'What is this babbler trying to say?' Others remarked, 'He seems to be advocating foreign gods.' They said this because Paul was preaching the good news about Jesus and the resurrection.*"
> - Acts 17:18 (NIV)

Bible translators could not have rendered this verse to state Paul was "*advocating foreign demons,*" otherwise they would have been branded him a heretic. So, in the above passage, the word *daimonion* is translated correctly as "gods;" but in I Corinthians Chapter 10, the same word is purposely, incorrectly translated as "demons," or even "devils" in some Bibles:

> "*No, but the sacrifices of pagans are offered to demons, not to God, and I do not want you to be participants with demons.*" - I Corinthians 10:20 (NIV)

The Apostle Paul, who wrote the chapter from which the above passage was excerpted, was concerned about idolatry, which is the worship of false gods.

Staying within that context, it makes much more sense that the correct translation should have been rendered "gods" in place of "demons." Paul wanted believers to believe in one god, not many gods. This is just one small example of how demons were erroneously inserted into the New Testament by Bible translators. By doing so, they were able to create passages that seemed to support nefarious church doctrines.

Again, it is important to understand that the original meaning of the Greek word *daimon* (and its derivations), as written in many of the books of the New Testament, was transformed over two millennia into today's current beliefs concerning devils and demons. If we were to look further at other passages containing the word *daimonion* in the Gospels, we would see that the meaning is sometimes synonymous with the translation of "unclean spirit" in some scriptures (Compare Mark 1:23 with Luke 4:33, for example.). An unclean spirit would be very similar to the original Greek meaning of the word *daimones*. Yeshua, we read, spoke to the unclean spirits and they obeyed, leaving the people they possessed. This is important to grasp, because we also read in the Bible that Yeshua taught that all of us should look to be clean and pure within. For example, in Matthew 23:26, we are told that Yeshua scolded the Pharisees to "...*clean the inside of the cup and dish first, so that the outside might also become clean.*" The whole idea of clean and unclean has more to do with the condition within the heart of mankind, and whether or not our thoughts are grounded upon truth. We are to be pure of Spirit by simply following the truth received from the divine guide within us. This eventually negates the leadership of the ego and the allure of its impure thoughts and ideas. Basically, we cast out incorrect thinking by simply following truth.

I would like to also touch on another idea regarding *daimones*, *daimonion*, and the idea of unclean spirits leaving people. What if unclean spirits were more than just thoughts, being the spirits of people? As I shared in the previous chapter, most near death experiences share the common thread of a "life-review," which appears to be a "cleansing process within," in order to help the recently-deceased transition from the physical world into the next. This experience often occurs after entering a tunnel of light and meeting loved ones on the other side of the grave. Perhaps, until the soul (or spirit) of a person progresses through to this light (tunnel) and cleansing process, the soul is somewhat darkened due to lack of understanding. The person finds their self being a lost, unclean spirit, as the light (truth) that is hidden within them is temporarily covered, like placing a basket over top of a candle. I am suggesting that the unclean spirits found within the Bible could also serve as descriptions for lost, human spirits. Perhaps, these disembodied humans were he *daimonion* Yeshua instructed to cease from clinging to people and the earthly life, encouraging them to move on unto the light and life-review. We read Yeshua, a Jewish radical, was questioned about this new way of dealing with spirits after he cast some out while within a Jewish synagogue in Capernaum. It should be noted that disembodied human spirits becoming attached to another person in the physical realm was not a new idea to Jewish believers. Conversing with spirits and instructing them to leave, however, was certainly brand new! All of this may sound a bit far-fetched, but if we are eternal then all of us are connected and part of the whole Spirit. Every person, then, will need to be completely freed from self-created, incorrect thinking which is figuratively described as "uncleanness." We need to train our minds to accept the idea that all people are relevant, whether they have a visible body or not. We are connected with one another more than we know.

Perhaps, we need to understand Yeshua's culture and the Jewish beliefs regarding ghosts a bit better. In Jewish folklore, a wandering soul (spirit of a deceased human) is known as a *dybbuk*. The word *dybbuk* means "clinging" or "cleaving." It was believed that the soul of a person sometimes remains behind after death of the physical body, and at times seeks attachment to another living human being for a mutual purpose, until the *dybbuk* can move on in his or her own life journey. A *dybbuk* is just another word for a *ghost*, an earthbound spirit. When one compares the Greek *daimones* with the Jewish *dybbuk*, one similarity stands out: both are described as having a dual-nature capable of both good and bad behavior. Human beings also share this same nature of free will, having the ability to choose between what is perceived to be right or wrong, and acting accordingly. In the Jewish scriptures of I Samuel, we read about a negative spirit that attaches to King Saul to trouble him:

> *"Saul's attendants said to him, 'See, an evil spirit from God is tormenting you. Let our lord command his servants here to search for someone who can play the harp. He will play when the evil spirit from God comes upon you, and you will feel better."* - I Samuel 16:15-16 (NIV)

This is an example of a *dybbuk* (a clinging human spirit) in the Old Testament of the Bible, and indicates that spirit attachment is possible according to Jewish scriptures. What is interesting is that the negative spirit is said to come from God. Perhaps the word "evil" in the above passage would be better translated as "negative," for an evil spirit would never come from a good God, could it? I suggest to you that this spirit was a human spirit that simply chose to behave poorly. I share this because the religious culture surrounding Yeshua is important to understand. Being a Jewish Rabbi, he was surely aware of such teachings, and I suspect the real Jesus knew how to minister to people on both sides of the grave. Possibly, Yeshua understood the condition of lost human spirits, and what it would take to redeem them.  Today, Rabbis experienced in practical Kabbalah still perform rituals to help both the afflicted, as well as the clinging human spirit.  It is claimed that many times, the attachment is often due to unfinished business here on Earth.

You may wonder how human spirits could possibly remain with those of us here on Earth.  Know that all of us are spirits within Spirit, so there can never be separation from each other.  Perhaps, we simply need to reconsider our current beliefs.  For maybe some of us are wrongly calling the earthbound spirits of people "demons."  And if such spirits are lost, it is because they do not yet understand who they are, unaware of their inseparable connection to the Divine.  Is it possible that Christianity has kept us from understanding our spiritual condition by promoting fear and falsehoods, having done a great injustice to countless thousands of people?  I wonder...

# 6 Religion & Church versus Spirituality

At this point, you must think I'm very critical of Christianity and unable to find any redeeming virtues within religion as a whole.  And if I am to be honest, I have also questioned that perhaps my opinion may be too critical.  In consideration of this, I have sought to identify any redeeming qualities of religion.  Does religion have any value at all?  I have come to the conclusion, after experiencing my own spiritual freedom, there is indeed evidence that religion can be utilized as a tool that eventually might help to remove religious ideals from within a person.  For without me delving into religion, while searching for answers to life's questions, I possibly would not have encountered the revelation of Spirit that changed my life.  In retrospect, the ritualistic worship, prayer and Bible studies truly gave me something to now reflect upon for comparison.  I find myself constantly thinking about my former beliefs in order to better understand why I was lured into religion.  Even though I am cynical toward much of Christianity's teachings, I truly am appreciative that religion grants people the opportunity to enjoy friendships within a local assembly of like-minded seekers.  In fact, I applaud the existence of Christian communities with positive influence consisting of non-exclusive, non-condemning, ever forgiving, always loving, and tirelessly giving congregations.  A few such non-dogmatic, Christian groups come to mind, like the

*Association of Unity Churches,* the *Unitarian Universalist Association of Congregations,* and *The Church of Christ, Scientist* branch churches and societies. Such churches, that promote spirituality in pursuit of truth, can be of great value to those who are fortunate to be a part of them.

Still, with all the positives considered, it is pertinent we acknowledge that many people do not yet understand the difference between religion and spirituality. Many believe they are one and the same. In fact, someone in my life recently pointed to scientific research indicating that being involved in religion can help people live healthier lives. Therefore, many believe religion to be a good thing. Though there are a few positives found within religion at times, often these institutions demand more from people than they give. The very word "religion" likely evolved out of *religare,* which means *"to restrain; tie back."* *Restraining* the minds of people is the purpose behind religious ideas. Conversely, spirituality truly allows one to be free. Membership within religious organizations often requires adherence to the teachings of false ideas created by men, not God, in order to control. Subscribing to the same ideals allows one to become a member of the private club, so to speak. Many religions, especially traditional Christianity, want us to join it, be a part of the system, and pledge allegiance to what the group considers sound, core tenets of their specific faith. In other words, if the majority believes it, it is validated as being true; or so the assembly believes. There is no place in such a closed society for those who disagree. People who disagree are considered to be lost souls, obvious outcasts before God. Derogatory labels and avoidance by friends are prices paid by those who choose to think for themselves.

In order to gain and restrain people, religion has been responsible for numerous wars. Wars are often initiated because someone demands something from another. Similarly, harmful religion always demands converts to subscribe to its doctrines, no matter how heretical. A battle is therefore waged by many religious institutions in order to overpower the minds of people. Should a person choose to not support the religion's teachings, there is no hesitation in letting him or her know he or she is in trouble with God. The idea of God is used to control those within the religious system, sort of like a big bouncer watching over the entire group. Nobody wants to be beaten up or tossed out, so adherence to the rules, or common beliefs, seems like a very good idea. I wish to emphasize the word *beliefs*, because that is what religion requires: believing in something that is learned from another. As previously mentioned, *belief* is a form of fear, because it has an air of doubt. *Knowing*, on the other hand, is not a form of fear, and thus empowering. Religion always works to keep its believers in control, and it does so by instilling fear as it is associated with *belief*. *Faith* is just a sugar-coated word used in place of *belief*. Fear is easily created by asking people to believe in things outside of themselves for answers. The Christian religion, for example, asks followers to put their faith in a God who is external and separate from them; a Heaven located upward; the worship of God from within an adorned building that appears godly; a communion of wine (or juice) and bread; the words of an Almighty God being contained within a book; a Hell situated down below; and a gruesome, sacrificially humble death (represented by a cross). These examples are nothing more than distractions designed to entertain the minds of people, ever keeping them busy. Such elements (and many others) of the Christian church are used to teach people to find life's answers from things that are external, temporal, and unfortunately of little, or no value. Remember that everything outside of us will eventually pass away, while only Spirit is eternal.

External, religious devices distract us from following the true path within. The word *distraction* means "*to cause mental confusion.*" One who is truly spiritual never focuses solely on the physical world for answers, for what wisdom can be found amidst chaos? To be spiritual means we look to Spirit for direction. By doing so, we seek to follow the leading of the voice within our heart, for the voice of Spirit can only be divined from *within* the person. True spirituality is about finding life's answers from *within*, which is contrary to the *visible me*. The *visible me*, or ego, is incapable of receiving direction from the inner source, for the ego was falsely created by ignoring it altogether. While the devices of religion might feed the need and greed of the ego (the fearful, false you), spirituality effectively silences the ego by not allowing it to maintain control through attachment to the outside environment. Religion was created by the ego, so its lessons are imperfect, only seeking to validate untruths. Therefore, the ego must find a way to resolve the problem it created: the separation between it and God. Since the ego fears eternal separation from God, which means its death (revealing the ego is not real), it mistakenly creates religion as an escape, relying on it for a hopeful rescue. Some may wonder if there is evidence of this struggle written anywhere within the Bible. We read Yeshua pointed out that there are indeed two people within us:

> *"Whoever tries to keep his life will lose it, and whoever loses his life will preserve it. I tell you, on that night two people will be in one bed; one will be taken and the other left. Two women will be grinding grain together; one will be taken and the other left."* - Luke 17:33-35 (NIV)

The ego will pass away one day, for it is a separate, false identity that will begin to lose power after the physical body passes. The ego therefore fears its own mortality. If there is something it can do to appease God, then the ego will find a way to get back into the deity's good graces in the hope of salvation. This may sound ludicrous, but the ego can only interpret the world outside of it. Therefore, the idea of a deity capable of providing a rescue plan is its only hope. In most forms of Christianity, we learn God is pleased when we accept the blood sacrifice of Jesus as our atonement. By doing so, the *visible me* believes it is now safe, and remains in control. However, the *visible me* is an artificial self that truly believes it is real; whose existence depends on our believing it's who we really are. The ego feels lost, threatened, worried, and unworthy because it has no credibility. When we lose our identity by believing in the ego, we mentally align ourselves with the same thoughts of self-condemnation, not believing we are indeed worthy. One might think, "*I am a happy person, and do not feel condemned.*" If this is true, then one should never have need for traditional Christianity or its method of salvation. Should we choose to believe we need God to save us, it is because we falsely believe the ego's lie that we are less than perfect and in a condition of disrepair.

Yeshua, we read, described the difference between following a religion and being spiritual this way:

> "*Enter through the narrow gate. For wide is the gate and broad is the road that leads to destruction, and many enter through it.*" - Matthew 7:13 (NIV)

Many people believe religion, the broad road in the

above parable, is the easiest, quickest way to hopefully find spiritual answers. *"Surely, this is the most popular and best way to find God,"* they think. Like sheep, they find themselves following others over a cliff, unable to see the eventual destination. Ironically, this most convivial, appealing route to the heavens often leads nowhere. For many, religion frequently is responsible for mentally disconnecting a person from their source: Spirit. It does so by informing people they are lacking a connection with a being of higher intelligence, and are in dire need of rectifying this situation. This is where the fear begins. Spirituality, on the other hand, will lovingly reveal that we are *already* connected, always have been and always will be. Once a person fully understands this within their deepest being, the realization of never being lost and always found is quite comforting. This is peace. Connection with Spirit is simply a matter of learning to regard the voice already within the person. This tiny, hidden path to the eternal may be difficult for us to recognize, but has never been far away; for it is always right in our midst - *within*. Therefore, our true self desires to be found. Spirituality is the true, narrow gate that few easily find; but those who find it are rewarded with life and truth. Our deepest fear can no longer have a foothold, for should the ego attempt to re-introduce the false idea of disconnection, all one has to do is search inwardly to remember our unbreakable union with the eternal source, which only seemed lost for the moment. We may find ourselves lost in our thoughts temporarily; but only if we choose to accept the lies of separation that religion promotes.

Religion, such as Christianity, is not new. Religious ideas can be traced back to tribal cultures who worshiped gods they feared, in order to appease them. If a natural disaster occurred, such as an earthquake, then superstitious tribesmen would claim God was angry. Of course, this angry deity would need to be pacified; otherwise, his wrath would likely be experienced again. This type of early religious belief is known as *animism*. Religion, such as animism, seems to always be adept at identifying angry gods hiding somewhere outside the village. The Christian religion is no different. Christianity teaches that all of us are born as sinners, destined to be condemned to an eternal place of punishment by one angry God. Christians are taught, "*Vengeance is mine...sayeth the Lord*" (excerpted from Romans 12:19 KJV). After learning the wicked are to be punished eternally, we are then informed this same angry God thankfully devised a rescue plan to save as many people as possible. Christianity teaches if we believe in Jesus as being the blood sacrifice for our sins (in order to satisfy this blood-thirsty deity), God will then save us from a place named Hell. This plan of salvation sounds very similar to animism, the most ancient of religions, doesn't it? Do we really want to believe that we need to pacify an angry God in order to escape his wrath? Those who fearfully choose to believe Christianity's nonsense are immediately cast into an emotional hell.

Let's explore the rise of the Christian church, once again. Today, many people believe that Christianity, and what we may call church, was started by Jesus. But the early church did not gather within church buildings, nor did early Christians admire beautiful religious statues, stained glass, or such elaborately decorated places of worship. Christians in the first few centuries met in homes that were large enough to accommodate a small group of people. This meant that persons who hosted the early gatherings of fledgling believers were mostly wealthy, literate leaders who were capable of reading aloud various Christian texts of the time. Remember, there were no denominations, offering plates, Bibles, hymnals, Sunday school classes, or programs to entertain worshippers. After Yeshua's crucifixion, the stories and ideas surrounding him varied. Yeshua was misunderstood, and his story controversial. Followers of Yeshua were not organizationally united, and thus believed different things about him and his ministry. Christianity was not created by Yeshua; but over time, Jesus was created by Christianity. Even his name was manufactured by the proponents of Orthodox Christianity. Men promoted their teachings and ascribed them to a man they coined as "Jesus," never allowing the true man's message to come forth. The man's name was Yeshua. He was a Jewish radical who spoke against ignorant, religious leaders of his time. He also related wonderful spiritual messages by way of parables: stories that contain spiritual truths. Yeshua didn't build a church building, take offerings, establish communion, write the New Testament, or promote any other religious ideals that we know of. Men who came after Yeshua, however, did indeed establish such ideals, eventually crafting a religion loosely based upon him that is now known as Christianity.

Much of early Christianity is a complicated story of an unorganized religion with varying beliefs. In short, there were three primary groups of Christians out of many that emerged after Yeshua's death: Gnosticism, Jewish Christianity, and Orthodox Christianity. Gnostic Christians sought to cast away the teachings of Judaism in preference to what Yeshua taught. They believed Yeshua introduced them to the better, higher God who would restore man to his former, perfect state through sheer knowledge (*gnosis* is Greek for *knowledge*). Gnostics taught that man's condition of struggle was a result of the destructive, imperfect God of Judaism, who created a substandard, material-based world. In stark contrast, Jewish Christians followed this God of Judaism, accepting much of the Hebrew Law of Moses. Jewish Christians simply chose to incorporate Yeshua's teachings of non-violence and simple living into their beliefs, while not accepting the need for bloody sacrifices. Orthodox Christianity, on the other hand, attempted to merge the teachings of Judaism with Orthodox Christian ideas by claiming Jesus was the Old Testament God in the flesh, having fulfilled the Law of Moses by offering himself as the final sacrifice for the world.  These groups, as well as other types of Christians, debated their differences in belief quite passionately.  Letters from many different perspectives were written in order to promote the various beliefs concerning Yeshua, and what his message meant to them.  It took a few centuries for Orthodox Christianity to finally prevail over other prominent doctrines, and it did so by becoming an official, state-created, and approved religion of the Roman Empire.  For self-serving interests, government not only validated and empowered the Orthodox view, but nurtured it through money and influence.  It's important I reiterate that Yeshua (Jesus) did not invent Christianity or the Church, as many Christians today believe.  What many call "*the Church*" was founded by councils of men who had never met Yeshua.  They formally began establishing the doctrines we know today, at the Council of Nicaea, roughly three hundred years after Yeshua's earthly life.  Over time, the Orthodoxy primarily adopted teachings of the Apostle Paul, who never personally knew Yeshua either.  More importantly, Paul was considered a heretic by many Jewish Christians of the time.  Therefore, Jewish Christians rejected Paul's teachings, which ironically later became part of Orthodox doctrines.  Yet, they were the most likely group of Christians to have actually known Yeshua and heard his real messages. Orthodox Christianity altered and even added text to manuscripts in order to deify Jesus, essentially creating documented support for their version of Yeshua's life and purpose. Ideas of Jesus' virgin birth, his resurrection from the dead, and of course his divinity are all of Orthodox design. By promoting Paul's letters, along with other edited documents (the Bible), the Orthodox Church grew into a religion for the Gentiles (the non-Jewish), while Yeshua and those with whom he interacted were Jewish. Regrettably, other beliefs regarding Yeshua would eventually succumb to the Western creation of Christianity which grew in power and popularity. Christianity is therefore primarily a Western religion, although it claims its roots in the Middle East, specifically from within Judaism.

These Orthodox Church teachings of Jesus eventually became Roman Catholicism which would later spawn many different Christian sects and denominations. Today, the different Christian organizations are nearly infinite, each of them varying some way in their beliefs and practices. They include *Anglican, Apostolic, Assemblies of God, Baptist, Bible, Byzantine Catholic, Catholic, Christian Science, Church of Christ, Church of the Brethren, Eastern Orthodox, Episcopal, Evangelical, Friends, Grace Brethren, Lutheran, Nazarene, Pentecostal, Presbyterian, Reformed Baptist, Southern Baptist, United Church of Christ,* and *United Methodist* for example. The list can go on and on. The fact that there are differences between all of them shows us two things:

1) The sheer number of different Christian organizations demonstrates that Yeshua's message has been greatly misunderstood by many.

2) Yeshua's message must truly have been important and influential in order to create such a fuss.

It is apparent that Yeshua made an impact on many. He must have said something that was worth listening to. But what was his message? Perhaps we can understand what Yeshua was doing by piecing together a different picture from what the New Testament Gospels tell us. By doing so, some very important details should become apparent. First, and foremost, Yeshua never created a religion in his name. Nowhere within the four Gospels can we find any stories indicating that Yeshua desired to begin a religion we now call Christianity. Actually, we can read numerous examples in the Bible of Yeshua speaking against religion and the religious leaders of his day. He never condemned the common man or woman but seemed to consistently direct harsh words toward religious leaders who sought to control people; especially those profiting from others' spiritual ignorance. In one example, Yeshua overturned the money tables within the Jewish temple. This was an obvious display of his distaste for a corrupt religion receiving monetary gain. It seems that most religious institutions are seldom satisfied by simply acquiring converts. They play the game of making the congregation feel guilty, in order to receive donations of money and time. Once minds are captured through fear, they can then be used for the institution's agenda by its religious leaders.

Because Yeshua spoke against such practices, he often was confronted by religious leaders. They did so, in order to attempt to silence him. The Gospels reveal that the leaders of the Jewish religion would often cite Hebrew scriptures in order to affirm they were following God's will (sound familiar?), while attempting to discredit Yeshua. In return, Yeshua also quoted Hebrew scriptures in order to counter leader's claims of being God's emissaries, revealing their hypocrisy. By doing so, he was able to help some of the Jewish community relinquish the religious fears created by ancient Judaism's legalistic teachings. If we read closely, we notice Yeshua directed much opposition toward corrupt religious leaders, for it was they who created fear in others through their error-ridden doctrines. Christianity would like us to believe that much of Yeshua's condemning words were spoken against mankind as a whole, but this simply is not true.

Let's further consider the New Testament picture of Yeshua's life. We read in the Bible that Yeshua walked through villages and countryside while people followed to hear him speak. His words were delivered in parable and power. He amazed communities, as he spent time demonstrating true love to those who were previously spiritually broken by Jewish religious leaders. Yeshua never verbally attacked the common people; otherwise, they would never have been eager to follow him. He did, however, speak against religious leaders of his day who were burdening these same people.

Yeshua related his messages through parables, so that spiritually dead, religious leaders, who could only literally interpret written laws and scriptures, would not be able to grasp the true, hidden, spiritual meanings found within his metaphorical stories. Thus, we read in the Gospel of Matthew that Yeshua stated,

> *"This is why I speak to them in parables: 'Though seeing, they do not see; though hearing, they do not hear or understand.'"* - Matthew 13:13 (NIV)

Yeshua's words of truth are a figurative, spiritual message that needs to be understood *within* one's inner being. This means to correctly understand his parables, it requires being able to recognize the hidden interpretation that rings true deep inside of us. Religious leaders struggled, however, to comprehend a teaching that was not of a literal or legalistic explanation. They were more comfortable with rules and practices. To them, everything they understood about God had more to do with physical events, observances and rituals. If God were to establish a Kingdom on Earth to rule over mankind, then he would do so by sitting upon a throne within a temple somewhere in the physical world. Jewish religious leaders asked Yeshua when God's Kingdom would come upon the Earth. In response, Yeshua explained that the reign of God is not some external, future event:

> "...*The Kingdom of God is not going to be observed coming, and people will not say, 'Here it is,' or 'There it is,' because the Kingdom of God is within you.*" - Luke 17:20-21

Yeshua taught that the Kingdom of God is already within each of us. Consequently, God's reign neither would be found outside of one's self, nor could it be seen happening with physical eyes. The Kingdom is the invisible Spirit. Spirit speaks within the heart of each individual, for Spirit *is* the heart of mankind. One can only imagine Yeshua's message having caused some listeners to finally realize, "*Who needs a religion to interpret what God is saying, if the voice of Spirit is already speaking to us directly? We just need to heed the voice of the Divine inside of us.*" Yeshua's ideas were a direct attack against religious instruction that relies upon outward buildings, outward worship, outward prayers, outward laws, and outward leaders. Such devices of religion are used to divert one's attention to anywhere but inward. A message against Judaism's dogma eventually led to the physical death of Yeshua, in order to silence him.

After Yeshua's crucifixion, confusion permeated the minds of his followers. As various notions concerning him spread, men still worked hard to organize one religion in his place. Many misunderstood Yeshua's ideals, however, so this made it difficult for people to agree upon what his sayings meant. This is why it took hundreds of years for one form of organized Christianity to emerge. As I touched on previously, the teachings of Jesus' virgin birth, resurrection, and that he was God in the flesh were all creations of the early, Orthodox form of Christianity. These doctrines were constructed in order to deify Jesus. By doing so, it merged the history of Judaism into Christianity by simply making Jesus into the radical, new form of the old, Hebrew God. Doctrines were easy to establish by either creating new manuscripts, or simply changing existing manuscripts in order to make them convey desired ideas. With most of the ancient world illiterate, only a very small percentage of the population would have been capable of examining religious writings. Let's explore just one of the biggest crimes in biblical manuscript manipulation, found in I John Chapter Five. This is the passage cited by the Church to substantiate their claims that the Father, Son and Holy Spirit are the triune God: God manifested in three different forms, also known as *The Trinity*:

"*For there are three that bear witness in heaven:*

*the ather, the Word, and the Holy Spirit; and these three are one. And there are three that bear witness on earth:   the Spirit, the water, and the blood; and these three agree as one.  If we receive the witness of men, the witness of God is greater; for this is the witness of God which He has testified of His Son."*
- I John 5:7-9 (NKJV)

Unfortunately, the phrase, *"in heaven: the Father, the Word, and the Holy Spirit; and these three are one.  And there are three that bear witness on earth,"* was added in the preceding passage by scribes hundreds of years later to provide scriptural support of the Trinity doctrine.  By causing people to believe that examples, such as this, are truthful, the Church worked diligently to turn Yeshua into a god who is to be worshiped.  This is just one of many examples of how Christianity was crafted, well after Yeshua's time on Earth.  Despite thousands of years of Christianity's attempts to solidify their story of Yeshua in order to satisfy any scrutiny, the flaws within the manuscripts and Church doctrines are still very visible to those who dare examine them.

The Orthodox, Christian Church sought to lay its foundational teachings primarily upon the Epistles of the Apostle Paul.  By doing so, Paul gave the Church a list of things Christian followers should and shouldn't do.  In other words, Orthodox Christian leaders wanted legalistic doctrines, and Paul's letters asked his followers to strictly conform to his religious principles. The Pauline Epistles provided growing, Orthodox Christianity just what it was looking for; and with a little manipulation of New Testament manuscripts, doctrines could be cemented which would further the Church's authority. The Church also grew with the finances and strength of the government and also due to the fact that it was a benefactor of conquests. It's unbelievable, really, that such a conflicting, corrupt organization could be built upon the reputation of one man who ironically promoted pacificism, spiritual freedom and inner peace. Do Christians really understand who Yeshua was?

Today, the Christian Church has many denominations, sects and divisions created through differences in doctrine, yet Christians still claim to represent Jesus' message to the peoples of the world. I wonder, with so many interpretations of Yeshua, which message we are to believe? It is apparent that what we call "Christianity" is just another man-made religion, expanding, evolving, ever-dividing, and never truly healing anyone. It's focus is materialistic, though disguised as being spiritual in nature. Many church congregations today are focused upon amassing numbers of people and providing entertaining programs in order to raise money. By raising more money, more programs can be created, and more people can be acquired. It is the popular Christian belief that by entertaining, God's kingdom will expand through their efforts. The thought process is: build it, and the people will come. Larger congregations called mega-churches openly display their success and excess by building huge gymnasiums, worship centers with stadium seating and other examples of top-shelf attractions, all in the name of Jesus. Christianity has now grown into quite an entertainment company, with movies, music, theme parks and more. Being religiously entertained does not make one spiritual. However, it is fortunate that spirituality may coincidently be found while on this path of trying to find religion. Much of Christianity, unfortunately, injures people by not revealing who they truly are, rarely helping them to become spiritually awakened. Entertainment is distraction, and if someone is looking for truth, distraction often diverts one's attention away from finding answers.

Though entertaining, I reiterate religion can be harmful in that it prolongs one's own suffering. Allow me to summarize the flawed message of most of Christianity and how it casts people into a cycle of suffering. The Christian church, in general, asks people to look to both their past and future in order to keep them focusing on what does not exist. By doing so, people are mentally held captive to something they are powerless to change. If people fear their past, they cast doubt on their future. Not surprisingly then, people are told that their only relief from past mistakes will be found by following an escape plan to dodge the future wrath of God. When examined closely, such teachings are nothing more than a crafty way to take possession of followers emotionally. When people fear their past mistakes, they naturally are moved to try and fix what they believe is a horrible future. Their hopes of escape are then placed upon what the Church teaches as a plan of salvation: an angry God will spare those who ask forgiveness and accept His only Son as a sacrifice in their place. The problem with this, as mentioned before, is that the fear Christianity created will not be gone after accepting their salvation plan (though it may feel alleviated at the time). Salvation implies being delivered from eternal separation from God. To the contrary, Christians were never separate from Spirit (God), although after hearing the Heaven versus Hell message of the Church, they believed they were. How can one be delivered from separation if we were never separate to begin with?

Our true atonement, or reconciliation with God, is when we realize we are already one with Spirit and not lost. We can never be cast away from Spirit: knowing this is "at-one-ment." Being in-tune with Spirit *is* reconciliation with God. If there is any forgiveness needed, it is we who must learn to forgive ourselves. This is the beginning of salvation, in my opinion. As long as we hold ourselves in a state of condemnation, believing we are bad people deserving punishment, how can we ever truly feel worthy? As long as we think we are unworthy, will we ever feel whole and at peace? Surely, we will not. No matter how big a sacrifice could be made by another in our stead (such as Jesus dying on the cross), we would never be clean inside until we know we are worthy. We are the creators of our own mental state; therefore, we are ultimately responsible for our own restoration.

I never knew peace as a Christian, though I thought for a time that I was at peace.  Then I realized that the world for me became one of loss, with so many family members and friends destined for eternal punishment.  I looked at the past, and saw a frightening future for myself and so many.  One day, I realized that if others were not free, how could I ever be?  It seemed that peace was unobtainable for me. For years I continued to fall short as I counted my errors, until I finally realized my past, as well as my mistakes were gone.  The past was over and done. Why fret over something that cannot be relived? Sure, I may not have been happy with some choices I made, but did I learn from them?  If so, then the past had value and meaning, no matter how painful.  We must learn to embrace the present, forgive ourselves and others by forgetting the past, and not try to live our lives focused on the future.  We must live in the moment to live fulfilling lives of true inner peace.  It's been said to be heavenly-minded makes one no earthly-good.  There's some truth to that.  Hopefully, you will know that only today, right now, is real. Seek spirituality, and not religion, by looking within to the Spirit.  Today is the day to find freedom and peace.

# 7 Yeshua & The Kingdom Message

When I reflect upon my life, I realize a large part of it has been spent mulling over various ideas concerning Yeshua. At times I have felt my pursuits have produced more questions than answers. All of this has caused me to wonder, "*Do we even know this man we call Jesus?*" Realizing that much of what many believe about the man has been misconstrued, I often ask myself, "*Where do we go from here?*"

Who was Jesus? That is the question. Better yet, who was Yeshua? We have accounts of him found within the four Gospels and other writings, but does anyone within Christianity today understand what Yeshua's life exemplified? For many Christians, Jesus is God in the flesh, but I do not believe that was what Yeshua would want us to believe. I cannot find within the New Testament where the man, many call Jesus, sought to be worshiped and revered as God Almighty. And should we find such a verse within the Bible which could be somehow interpreted as such, I am not certain we could trust that it had not been added into the text by the creators of Orthodox Christianity in order to provide additional support of their theology. As previously mentioned, most all forms of Christianity eventually spun off of these Orthodox teachings that were established first. Even though various sects and denominations of Christianity may differ in doctrine and ritual, they still share many of the same basic fundamental flaws of the original Orthodox creation. Variations within Christianity primarily arose out of differing ideas about Yeshua and his message; dissensions often being products of disparate Bible interpretations. Reading this, one might wonder, "*Which form or group found within Christianity is correct?*" I would ask the reader to consider that maybe none of them are correct, as most all forms of Christianity were founded on false premises. In one way or another, the monopoly of Orthodox ideas have influenced nearly every group within Christianity, making it almost an impossible task to decipher the true message of Yeshua. For me, trying to comprehend the man's real message had been a struggle, but eventually my search for truth became a personal journey of attempting to discern what I am hearing deep within me.

It has become evident that the Christian church was simply founded upon manuscripts. These documents, many of which were created years after the death of Yeshua, were used to support strict, literal, Orthodox ideas. It was important for early Orthodox Christian leaders to find a way to portray, and subsequently prove, that Jesus was the Old Testament Hebrew God. Consequently, they needed to rewrite history in their favor. To do so, it required written proof of their doctrines. If passages within selected manuscripts, which later would be used to form the Christian Bible, did not support Orthodox ideas entirely, then they were merely amended by scribes. This is why the Apostle Paul's teachings, which are found in most of the New Testament Epistles, seem contrary to what we read Jesus taught in the Gospels. Hundreds of years before Orthodox Christianity put together its Bible, Paul had written letters to various communities in order to establish his own beliefs regarding Yeshua, even though he never knew him. Paul could only claim to know Yeshua through receiving visions of him. Still, Paul's letters, as well as letters written using his name, were heavily relied upon by Orthodox Christianity to fashion their specific brand of Christian religion.

As I touched upon previously, there were various Christian beliefs in the first century, as well as many who claimed to be apostles. There were also numerous early Christian manuscripts, such as other gospels, epistles, acts, and commentaries, which were written to promote different Christian views. Such manuscripts, opposing the Orthodox view, were simply cast away over time in order to establish one Christian theology. Texts, such as Paul's, were chosen and changed to more firmly support Orthodox views. Opponents were silenced, effectively setting in stone one interpretation of Yeshua for future generations. Eventually, Jewish, Gnostic, and most other forms of Christianity faded away as Orthodox Christianity gained power and influence through Rome's government. By manufacturing a book of history (the Bible) that purposely contained selected and altered manuscripts, Orthodox Christianity created Jesus, who we are to believe is the former Hebrew God revealed in human figure. Drawing from an ancient practice to embellish heroes, stories of his virgin birth and resurrection from the dead were also included in the book in order to make the deifying of Jesus complete.

Many early Christians did not believe Yeshua was the Hebrew God in flesh form, born from a virgin, and who later resurrected from the dead. However, we would never know this by reading the Bible alone. Early Jewish Christians taught that Yeshua promoted simple living and pacifism. Interestingly, they ascribed to communal-type living, vegetarianism, and believed Jewish scribes had altered the Hebrew manuscripts (the Bible's Old Testament) to include blood sacrifices of animals. They chose to follow the Law of Moses, ignoring the need for such sacrifices, and lived how they believed Yeshua had instructed them. In comparison, today many scholars of ancient manuscripts believe much of the Christian New Testament was also altered, with some of the manuscripts possibly even being forgeries. Similar to the Hebrew manuscripts, it would seem blood sacrifices were also woven into the Christian tale. Once Orthodox Christianity displaced all other versions, it became the primary story from which nearly all forms of Christianity would find their roots.

Christian teachings often work to focus our mind on

external things; likewise, so did the teachings of early, Jewish leaders during the time of Yeshua. By lacking spirituality, such religions inevitably create suffering, as they possess little truth. We learn this lesson when we read some of the passages attributed to Yeshua that dealt with the Orthodox, religiously-minded sects of Judaism, called the Sadducees and Pharisees:

> "...*Take heed and beware of the leaven of the Pharisees and of the Sadducees.*" - Mathew 16:6 (KJV)

> "*Woe to you, teachers of the law and Pharisees, you hypocrites! You travel over land and sea to win a single convert, and when he becomes one, you make him twice as much a son of hell as you are.*" Matthew 23:15 (NIV)

> "*Woe to you, teachers of the law and Pharisees, you hypocrites! You clean the outside of the cup and dish, but inside they are full of greed and self-indulgence. Blind Pharisee! First clean the inside of the cup and dish, and then the outside also will be clean.*" - Matthew 23:25-26 (NIV)

> "*Woe to you, teachers of the law and Pharisees, you hypocrites! You are like whitewashed tombs, which look beautiful on the outside but on the inside are full of dead men's bones and everything unclean. In the same way, on the outside you appear to people as righteous but on the inside you are full of*

*hypocrisy and wickedness."* - Matthew 23:27-28
(NIV)

There are many more passages within the Gospels
where we read about Yeshua battling religious
beliefs, but the above scriptures make the point that
religion is focused outwardly, indeed harmful, and
something Yeshua sought to lead people away from.
His battle and instruction against religion is very
important to understand, because it was key to his
message. To miss this is to not understand that
Yeshua directed people away from religion, teaching
them to seek their already established connection
with God found within. Eventually, this stand
against religion would ultimately lead to his death by
crucifixion. His physical death was important. It
showed followers that the body could be destroyed,
but who we truly are can never be touched, for we are
an eternal Spirit.

Unfortunately, the Judaism which Yeshua attacked
would not be the only religion culpable of
extinguishing people's spirituality. For men who
misunderstood Yeshua's teachings would, over time,
create Western Christianity in the name of Jesus,
claiming it to be the continuation of Judaism's Law of
reward and punishment. This new Christianity
would, of course, supersede the old Hebrew tradition
of following legalistic rules and sacrificial rituals,
essentially becoming more appealing to the masses.
Orthodox Christianity simply maintained that Jesus

fulfilled the former law by dying on the cross and becoming the sole, blood sacrifice needed in order to appease the blood-thirsty, Hebrew God, once and for all. In addition to explaining the purpose of Jesus' death in this manner, Orthodox proponents included a triumphant resurrection from the dead and ascension unto Heaven. Such depictions historically deified Jesus, misrepresenting him as the Supreme Being from Judaism. Hence, Jesus became Orthodox Christianity's God, a more personable visage who visited the Earth in flesh form. To make this idea more appealing, they needed to explain that Jesus was a physical materialization (the Son) of one of the three forms of God, otherwise taught as the Trinity: the Father, the Son and Holy Spirit. This way, God could still remain invisible, although he would now have a more acceptable, human form.

Due to such teachings, Christians today unfortunately focus on Jesus' death by remembering a cross of crucifixion, as well as a supposed resurrection from a tomb. By doing so, they are unable to comprehend Yeshua's true message that death is not real. And how could they, when his message has been altered; thereby, leading to today's existence of an abundance of false, religious institutions? To focus on death, or even the idea of resurrection, is to believe in illusion by placing too much value on the physical world. Death of the body can never harm the real you, which is Spirit. Something that is eternal can never cease to exist, and therefore never needs resurrection from the dead in the first place. I might suggest that if anything needs resurrected, it is the temporarily forgotten knowledge within us that we are eternal Spirit, incorruptible in nature. Many Christians are unable to recognize such a principle. Consequently, they are left feeling defeated, succumbing to suffering, and hoping for redemption sometime in their future:

> "*They know nothing, they understand nothing. They walk about in darkness; all the foundations of the earth are shaken. I said, 'You are gods; you are all the sons of the most high.'*" - Psalms 82:5-6 (NIV)

The above Old Testament passage sums up mankind's condition in general: we do not know who we truly are. The "earth" that is shaken, is a symbolic depiction of humanity. We read in the Hebrew scriptures (Genesis) that man is made from the dust of the ground. Adam, being formed from the Earth, illustrates the egocentric emphasis on the exterior, physical shell we call the body. By allowing our complete attention to be diverted away from our inner being, the mind becomes troubled and temporarily lost. In contrast to the earthy Adam of Genesis, Yeshua, referred to as the "second Adam" in the New Testament, revealed who we *really* are. Jesus is sometimes called the "Second Adam." The idea of a "second Adam" (or spirit man) is simply the representation of our hidden, inner being. Yeshua divulged that we should look within to the life-giving, powerful Spirit, the true person. By following this path, we will be able to recall the truth of our existence and manifest its fruits. We are already forever connected with supreme energy, and hence with each other, being empowered and not lacking. Many fail to recognize this.

Yeshua's message of the kingdom, related through parables, disclosed spiritual truths concerning humanity. He never taught that he was the supreme God, or that anyone was beneath him. In the New Testament, we can read how Yeshua demonstrated service to others, placing their needs above his own. He wanted to elevate our mind to understand that everyone is worthy and of the same, divine Spirit (just like him). This idea is definitely not what today's Christianity teaches, for Christian leaders want us to believe that Jesus was indeed *the* God manifested in physical form and someone to be worshiped. The support of their teaching is found within only a few verses of the Bible. Unfortunately, many of these passages were either added to manuscripts much later, altered, or composed in such a manner as to support the Orthodox, theological position. At the risk of sounding repetitive, it is important to remember that the idea of one God in three persons (the Father, the Son, and the Holy Spirit) was added to the New Testament by scribes. I John 5:7-8, the primary passage cited as reference to a triune-God, is not found in the earliest known Greek manuscripts. It was apparently added later to the Latin Vulgate, in order to support the Trinity doctrine that church leaders had created. Eventually, the addition made its way into English translations of the Bible's New Testament:

> "*For there are three that bear witness in heaven: the Father, the Word, and the Holy Spirit; and these three are one. And there are three that bear witness on earth: the Spirit, the water, and the blood; and these three agree as one.*" - I John 5:7-8 (NKJV)

The "*Father, the Word* (an obvious first century reference to Jesus) *and the Holy Spirit*" were added to demonstrate a God of three-persons; thus validating Jesus as being God. Something similar also happened to I Tim 3:16 where the word "god" should actually be translated as "who;" otherwise, it subtly turns Jesus into God:

> "*And without controversy great is the mystery of godliness: God was manifested in the flesh, justified in the spirit, seen by angels, preached among the Gentiles, believed on in the world, received up in glory.*" - I Timothy 3:16 (NKJV)

Another place in the New Testament where scribes changed text in order to deify Jesus can be found in Acts 20:28, where "church of god" should be rendered "church of the lord":

> *"Therefore take heed to yourselves and to all the
> flock, among which the Holy Spirit has made you
> overseers, to shepherd the church of God which He
> purchased
> with His own blood."* - Acts 20:28 (NKJV)

From just these few, well-known examples of biblical
manuscript manipulation, we can see how Jesus has
become the Christian church's God, unfortunately the
figurehead of a false religion. This may sound
harmless, but in truth it has propagated generation
after generation of people who do not know the truth
of who they are. On top of this, some have
succumbed to believing false, frightening ideas about
themselves and others. This is primarily due to
religion negatively influencing many of our
commonly-held, societal beliefs. Being a culprit,
Christianity has caused a large portion of humanity to
feel divided, lost and afraid.

Though Christianity has assigned Yeshua another
name and message, I still feel that the real man
understood and shared real truths that created quite a
stir two thousand years ago. So, we must ask
ourselves, *"What did he teach that was so radical at the
time?"* The closest we can get to what may have been
his real message, uncorrupted by religion, can be
discovered by looking at sayings which have been
attributed to him. Maybe, the words he spoke were
not completely spoiled through alteration,
mistranslation and incorrect interpretation. It is

possible Yeshua's secret sayings, as some have coined them, may have remained somewhat intact.  Their true, figurative meanings are largely misunderstood by many who, even today, seek to understand them by only a literal interpretation.  Having previously explained that Yeshua taught his followers through the use of parables, I will soon share a few of those sayings, found in the Bible, in order to unlock some of his Kingdom Message through figurative explanation. To know the truth, we each will have to rely upon our own inner witness of Spirit as the best guide to understanding Yeshua's teachings.

Knowing that Yeshua must have been enlightened with truth, I contemplated what many believe to be his teachings found within the Bible's Gospels.  I was attempting to comprehend them the way they were most likely meant to be understood when originally spoken.  The inner witness of Spirit guided me in this endeavor and began revealing some of the Bible's parables in a refreshing, new way.  Typically, I would hear certain spiritual truths within me first, before they were ever revealed to me within passages of the Bible.  I share this, so you understand that you do not need the Bible to know truth. Surely, if we are connected to the Divine through Spirit, then it is obvious that the truth is already within us.  We simply need to recall it, by allowing ourselves to tune-in and listen to what's inside our deepest being.  One must only choose to be willing to hear; then listen. When I say "hearing," I really mean *perceiving with spiritual ears,* which I describe as being a "knowing" within the heart. As mentioned before, I found that the biggest mistake Christians make, in attempting to understand the teachings of Yeshua, is that they interpret every Bible verse verbatim. To do so is a mistake, for Yeshua made it very clear, in several passages found within three of the four Gospels (Matthew, Mark, and Luke), that his teachings were simple stories that conveyed hidden spiritual truths (parables). If taken literally, the parables of Yeshua will not make sense, seem very frightening, and most importantly will not convey the truths of his Kingdom Message. For example, if Yeshua warned people about vipers, while confronting vile religious leaders of his day, would it make sense to believe he was describing an actual species of snake? Of course not. The vipers he spoke of would be an obvious reference to the religious leaders, and not a kind comparison at that.

To some, especially those who are ensnared by religion and have closed their minds, my words will fall on deaf ears. But to others, especially those who are desperately seeking truth and know something is amiss within the traditional Christian message, what I am writing will be of value. Many of Yeshua's spiritual concepts have been explained in previous chapters, but now it is time to bring it all together, summing up his core teaching. The book of Matthew details that Yeshua taught the common people *the gospel,* or "good news," of the kingdom. There is a stark contrast between Yeshua's real message and what Christianity claims Jesus taught. What Yeshua taught is more liberating, which is really good news! His message seemed simple, as he shared it within the synagogues, villages and countryside:

> *"From that time Jesus began to preach and to say, "Repent, for the kingdom of heaven is at hand."* - Matthew 4:17 (NKJV)

> *"And Jesus went about all Galilee, teaching in their synagogues, and preaching the gospel of the kingdom..."* - Matthew 4:23 (KJV)

Yeshua instructed those who listened, *"to repent."* *To repent*, simply implies to change one's mind; meaning *to think differently*. But what were listeners to think differently about? Yeshua asked people to reconsider the idea of a "Kingdom." "The Kingdom" does not literally imply a God coming and reigning upon the physical Earth sometime in the future, as some supposed. The Kingdom of God is actually the *reign of Spirit* within the hearts of mankind. In Matthew, this idea is called the *"Kingdom of Heaven,"* while similar passages in other Gospels are rendered the *"Kingdom of God."* It doesn't really matter too much which way it was written, for the words *Heaven* and *God* are synonymous with one thing: *Spirit*. Yeshua instructed people that they did not have to wait for heavenly, or godly things, to come, for all of it was at hand. As it was then, our connection to God and the heavens, namely Spirit, is accessible now.

To the Jewish people of Yeshua's day, it was important to believe that God would come and rescue them from the oppression of Rome. They waited for divine intervention, but many also relied upon priests to offer sacrifices to the Hebrew God in their stead. We must understand that the people Yeshua spoke to saw God as being something separate and distant from them. This concept of a disassociated God is not unlike Christianity's teaching of a disconnected deity. In stark contrast, Yeshua appeared on the scene proclaiming and demonstrating a relationship of oneness with God the Spirit, right in the peoples' midst. *"Was Yeshua to be the King of all Israel that God had ordained to not only rescue them, but reign over them in power? Would Yeshua, through divine authority, overthrow the evil Roman Empire?"* people wondered. To many Jews, *the Kingdom* meant God's Kingdom being established on Earth through a Messiah, a deliverer. They hoped and prayed for this deliverer to rescue them. Jewish followers must have questioned themselves and others, *"Could Yeshua be saying that he was the long-awaited Messiah who is here now to establish his Kingdom on Earth?"* The answer is, *"No."* For Yeshua to instruct the crowds about a Kingdom they could not physically see was confusing, to say the least. Some understood his message, but many did not. Yet, they knew there was something right about this man, whom they called *Yeshua*, the man we today call *Jesus*. So, the

fame of him, as well as his message, spread
throughout the area:

> "*Then Jesus went about all the cities and villages,
> teaching in their synagogues, and preaching the
> gospel of the kingdom...*" - Matthew 9:35 (KJV)

Soon, the popularity of Yeshua deemed it necessary
that he use his disciples to help further the good news
of the Kingdom:

> "*These twelve Jesus sent out and commanded them,
> saying: 'Do not go into the way of the Gentiles, and
> do not enter a city of the Samaritans. But go rather
> to the lost sheep of the house of Israel. And as you
> go, preach, saying, The kingdom of heaven is at
> hand.'*" - Matthew 10:5-7 (NKJV)

It is important to note that the same message Yeshua
began speaking, had now spread and was continually
being taught by him, as well as his disciples. He
never changed the theme of his discourse. The
Kingdom Message was what he sought to share with
as many people, as possible. Yeshua desired this
higher truth to spread, especially among his people,
the Jews. It was they, being shackled by the legalistic
teachings of Judaism, whom his heart longed to free
from religion. When many would not, or most likely
could not, comprehend the spiritual truths he shared,
Yeshua decided that the Kingdom Message should be
voiced to all manner of people; i.e., to anyone who

would listen. Again, the Kingdom Message was delivered in parables, and it confused the religious, Jewish leaders who struggled to comprehend what Yeshua was teaching:

> *"And the disciples came and said to Him, 'Why do You speak to them in parables?' He answered and said to them, 'Because it has been given to you to know the mysteries of the kingdom of heaven, but to them it has not been given. For whoever has, to him more will be given, and he will have abundance; but whoever does not have, even what he has will be taken away from him. Therefore I speak to them in parables, because seeing they do not see, and hearing they do not hear, nor do they understand.'"* - Matthew 13:10-13 (NKJV)

In the above passage, it is clear that the parables, the spiritual sayings of Yeshua, contain the hidden Kingdom Message that Christianity has sadly failed to comprehend. Some of us may even now perceive that modern Christian leaders, of most all denominations and affiliations, have made the same mistakes as their earlier Orthodox predecessors, with respect to misunderstanding the message of Yeshua. Let us not choose to continue down this same, mistaken path, for we can seek to learn his truths by simply considering the spiritual interpretation of sayings attributed to him. What was this *"message of the Kingdom"* that Yeshua and his disciples shared? The Kingdom Message is good to know, because it reveals important revelations about us that are life-changing and freeing. This *is* the real teaching for which Yeshua gave his life in order to share. It can be certain that the message of the Kingdom is not similar to any of the doctrines preached by the majority of Christian institutions over the last two thousand years. With it being impractical to list every parable Yeshua spoke, let's examine just a few very important passages found in the Gospels of John and Luke about the Kingdom:

> "...*Most assuredly, I say to you, unless one is born of water and the Spirit, he cannot enter the kingdom of God. That which is born of the flesh is flesh, and that which is born of the Spirit is spirit. Do not marvel that I said to you, You must be born again. The wind blows where it wishes, and you hear the sound of it, but cannot tell where it comes from and where it goes. So is everyone who is born of the Spirit.*" - John 3:5-8 (NKJV)

In the above passage, Yeshua mentions the breaking of water which occurs during childbirth, referencing the beginning of our physical existence. By doing so, he distinguishes between our natural birth, which all of us are surely aware of, and a second birth, something less-understood and of greater importance. He called this second birth, "*born of the Spirit.*" To be born of the Spirit means to simply awaken unto knowing that we are eternal Spirit. A spiritual re-birth needs to happen *within* everyone.

We need to be spiritually awakened. All of us are spirits within *the Spirit; i.e.,* something more than just a physical body. By knowing this, we can then turn our attention toward that deeper connection within us. The writer of John surely knew the importance of this when he wrote this gospel, for he shared Yeshua's words that describe what it's like to be aware of, and follow, the inner, guiding Spirit. This *Spirit*, which we are a part of *as spirits*, John further reveals to be God. We read that Yeshua clarified *what* God is, and how we relate with the deity:

> *"God is Spirit, and those who worship Him must worship in spirit and truth."* - John 4:24 (NKJV)

The author of John probably wrote such a gospel knowing that prior accounts of Yeshua's story were missing important truths of Yeshua's message, especially the Kingdom of God, the Spirit, being found within us. If we want to connect with the Divine, then we must understand that the Spirit which we all share is in fact the Supreme Being. It is the *Spirit* that is to reign within us. There is no other way to connect to the Divine, but by recognizing your part within the Deity, accepting it, and seeking to comprehend the truth of who you are. Looking to the divine source for direction *is* being born anew of the Spirit. By doing so, we enter into the Kingdom and allow the reign of God within us. Religion, especially Christianity, looks for God and a kingdom, even Heaven, to come to believers some day in their future.

By waiting for an external God and kingdom to hopefully come one day, we become unable to recognize the truth of our connection with Spirit, namely God, already. Yeshua warns not to listen to religious leaders who teach such wrongful ideas:

> *"Now when He was asked by the Pharisees when the kingdom of God would come, He answered them and said, 'The kingdom of God does not come with observation; nor will they say, See here! or See there! For indeed, the kingdom of God is within you.'"* - Luke 17:20-21 (NKJV)

Yeshua attempted to teach the curious religious leaders that the Kingdom of God is not something that is coming one day in their future. Furthermore, the Kingdom of God is not to be seen with our physical eyes on Earth; for the Kingdom of God is Spirit and can only be recognized and comprehended from within our hearts. We could sum up these passages by saying that Yeshua sought to reach those who were able to recognize the voice of Spirit. Still, most religious leaders could not hear his words, but only listened to him in order to try and condemn him through use of their religious law. They were unable to grasp that their religion was dead, as it mentally disconnected themselves, and others, from their true source - Spirit. These religious guides were unable to recognize that everyone is of one Spirit. They could only see themselves, and consequently others, as separated beings existing beneath an angry God, who must be pacified.  Numerous times, we read of them quoting scripture from the Jewish Law, in order to trap Yeshua.  He often responded back to such leaders with scriptures from their own, religious books, in ways that discredited their absurd teachings.

While writing this book, a gentleman e-mailed me with a very good observation.  He noted how we read in the Gospels (such as in Matthew, Chapter Five) that sometimes Yeshua quoted the Jewish Law, but would then spiritually clarify older passages by adding, "*but I say...*"  Yeshua would then expound upon such quotes from the Law, revealing a higher, spiritual truth that could be found within them, for people to ponder.  This allowed Yeshua to subtly transform the religious mind of people, by not attacking their beliefs, but expanding them.  This is most likely why we read that he stated:

> "*Do not think that I have come to abolish the Law or the Prophets; I have not come to abolish them but to fulfill them.*"  - Matthew 5:17 (NIV)

Yeshua used the religious obstacles he encountered, that stood in the way, to lead others unto a path of spirituality.  He wanted to move people beyond a book and dead religion, and unto spirituality and love.  He used scripture to not only answer his critics, but to confound the religious proponents around him.  For within the writings of the Hebrew Law and

Prophets, many thought truth, as well as their salvation, could be found. They were sorely mistaken. Just like the religious Jews of Yeshua's day, Christians also mistakenly rely upon a book for their salvation and knowledge. Both are unable to comprehend that God is not distant from them, or located somewhere outside of their being.

It is important I plainly state that many Christians wrongly believe Jesus is God, a deity to be worshiped in order to obtain salvation. Yeshua tried to get us to understand that this thinking was not correct. Do you remember when I previously shared Psalm 82:6, where it states, *"Do you not know that you are gods?"* We read that Yeshua quoted this old, Hebrew psalm, while undergoing public attack from religious leaders, due to teaching that the Spirit is within all of us, and all of us are within Spirit:

> *"Jesus answered them, 'Many good works I have shown you from my Father. For which of those works do you stone me?' The Jews answered him, saying, 'For a good work we do not stone you, but for blasphemy, and because you, being a man, make yourself God.' Jesus answered them, 'Is it not written in your law...you are gods? If he (the Father) called them gods, to whom the word of God came...do you say of me that I am blaspheming, because I say that I am the son of God? If I do not do the works of my Father, do not believe me; but if I do, though you do not believe me, believe the*

*works, that you may know and believe that the Father is in me, and I in him.'"* - John 10:32-38 (NKJV)

Yeshua's earthly life can best be described as being an example, a living portrait for us to observe. He demonstrated, for others to see, the power we have when we truly know who we are. By contemplating the stories surrounding his life, we can begin to understand the depth of our being. Yet, people naturally want to doubt their own connection to the Spirit, their Father, and rely on a man named Jesus to somehow overcome the woes of this world for them. This way of thinking is a form of escapism, a method to distract one from the real issue. They, who focus on another to rescue them, unintentionally diminish, in their mind, the power within them. Such a mind looks to Jesus, as an idol to be worshiped, in the hope of receiving a benefit in return. This type of thinking is analogous to a genie within a bottle. By putting faith in such a magical figment, many believe their wishes will be granted.

I'll ask the reader to consider this: What if the promise has always been in our midst, and we have simply failed to recognize it? If we choose to see Jesus as our deity, then we mentally, if not openly, worship an idol, clinging to the commercialized Jesus to solve life's issues. Knowing we are often the creators of our own suffering, where then is our responsibility in the matter? If we would only take a moment to step back and analyze much of our thinking, we would easily recognize fear motivating many of our decisions. By lacking understanding of the truth of who we are, we want to cling to another in desperate hope of salvation. Fear is the driving force behind desperation. I must ask the reader, *"Do you need rescued by another?"* If you do, then you likely remain unaware of what you need rescued from: the belief in fear. By being the creators of our condition, only we can end our cycle of suffering. No one can do the work for us. We allowed the mess, and so it is our responsibility to clean it up. Our path to freedom can undeniably be found through help of another, but only if such a person shares insights and leads by a loving example. Love is the antithesis to fear. It is love that eliminates fear, and love is found within every person's being. To receive love, we must look within to the source of love: Spirit. And that was the message within Yeshua's words and actions. In order to come to the Father, which means to recognize and communicate with Spirit, Yeshua emphasized we must do so *through his example*:

> *"Jesus said to him, 'I am the way, the truth and the life. No one comes to the Father except through me.'"* - John 14:6 (NKJV)

Yeshua demonstrated, in word and deed, that the method for communicating with his spiritual Father, is also how we need to connect with the higher power (God). The way to do this is by learning to recognize our own, personal link within the divine source. This path permits the inner voice to become our source for truth. We can read in the Bible where Yeshua stated *"God is Spirit,"* and that *"the Kingdom of God"* (the *reign of God*) *"is within"* us. Plainly spoken, the Spirit is who we are, and we need to trust this powerful guiding force inside us. The Spirit is like a true loving Father, one we can truly rely on. The meaning behind *"the way, the truth, and the life"* can be described as bringing forth true things, from deep within, through listening to the same Spirit that already energizes our existence. The Spirit is also nurturing and motherly. When one becomes aware and accepts this loving anointing of energy within, then by definition, this unity *is the Christ.*

Some believe Jesus and Christ to be the same thing. They may even think Christ was Jesus' last name. Paul, too, seemed to think that Christ was synonymous with Jesus, even though he (or more likely another author using his name) profoundly proclaimed in a letter to the Colossians:

> *"...Christ in you, the hope of glory!"* - Colossians 1:27 (KJV)

Christ is a description of one who lives by the inner guide of the anointing of Spirit. Operating as one with the life-force by following the inner voice, is to be Christ. This is the completion of the atonement, or *"at-one-ment"* (to be one with the Spirit). Such a person knows who they are, and relies upon the source of their existence to be their guide through life. The Apostle Paul, like the Christian religion built upon many of his (and others') writings, would like us to believe that only Jesus could be the Christ, the chosen anointed one. Confused, Paul and Christianity in general, instruct that we can receive communication from the Spirit (if we are saved believers), almost as if a spooky, Holy Ghost may visit us from time to time. This idea wrongly implies a disconnection from our source. Somehow, both failed to comprehend our already established union with God, even though we can discern from Yeshua's teachings that all of us are anointed, having our part within the divine Spirit. We need only to be reminded of this truth. By listening to the leading already found within us, we are immediately *in Christ*. We should know that all are valuable sons and daughters of God, for we have the Divine as our very being. That makes everyone descendants of the same Father of all spirits; *the Spirit* that all exist within. And if all of us are connected by one source, the Spirit, then we need to recognize that everyone, even everything, is connected. There truly is no separation; not from one another, or from God. Though I have given Paul some harsh criticism prior, I would like to think that even he may have partially grasped a bit of truth, when in Romans 8:14 we read:

> "*For as many as are led by the Spirit of God, they are the sons of God.*" - Romans 8:14 (KJV)

Several forms of Christianity teach that upon accepting Jesus as one's savior, the Holy Spirit is received by the believer as the indwelling Spirit of God. This Christian doctrine instructs that the Holy Spirit is needed to come and reside within a person in order for the Christian to be able to follow God's direction. In this teaching of exclusivity, converted Christians are taught they have the Holy Spirit dwelling within them. This wrongly implies that all others, specifically those who have not received Jesus as Lord, are incomplete and missing something. If we believe this to be true, then we must also believe there are many people existing as empty, human shells that have no part of God's Spirit within them. Many proponents of Christianity wrongly instruct such a thing, as though non-Christians are condemned, having no Spirit found within them, to begin with. When considered, this idea must be incorrect, for what is the life-giving energy that infuses everything? Wouldn't this energy be the Spirit, or God, in Christian terminology? Sure, it would have to be, because Christianity also teaches that only God gives life. The Spirit, the energy, that gives life to everyone and everything, *is* the same eternal Spirit that many call "God." It surely is plain to see that all people, animals and plants are alive. Something must animate them, correct? The Divine *is* the life-giving force that sustains all life. Everything that exists does so within the Divine Spirit and is a part of the whole. Though this is true, it still is possible for a person to be spiritually "dead" to the truth of who they are. Such persons remain unaware that they are more than a physical body, even though they are an eternal Spirit that is inseparable from the Divine.

*"The fear of the Lord is the beginning of wisdom"* is a Bible verse cited by many Christians to unwisely proclaim we need to fear an external God before we can be saved. This passage found in Proverbs 9:10, however, is often only half-quoted and is better understood as saying, *"Reverence of the eternal is the beginning of wisdom, and knowledge of the sacred is understanding."* When we understand that being fearful is not the intent of this verse (by looking at the original Hebrew), we then realize it conveys we should give heed to the eternal Spirit found within us that gives life and is who we really are. Therefore, Yeshua taught that we need to respect, and listen to, this inner voice of reason. For some, this is difficult to do, for they are completely unaware of their spiritual existence, and sadly, Christianity has not helped the matter. We need to understand that "God" and "Lord" are really only titles for the one Spirit, which none of us will ever become separated from. We are already in God.

Therefore, God is just a three letter word, and words mean different things to different people. The word "god," traditionally characterizes *"a deity who is greater than all, and someone who is separate from me."* To many, God is something that is located elsewhere, distant, and therefore disconnected from themselves. Christianity enhances this disconnection by constructing something false, an illusion, claiming we should see ourselves as being separated from God at birth. Religion then, promotes the idea that this very separation from God will be healed by accepting Jesus as one's Lord and Savior. We are taught to place our faith in his sacrificial death upon the cross, which we are told was done to reconcile us back to God. By doing so, we are then asked to believe we are securely linked to God, as evidenced by the gift of the Holy Spirit. If we choose to believe this "plan of salvation," or similar Christian doctrine, then *when* we make a mistake in our thinking (what Christians deem as sin), our connection with the Spirit will seem broken, appearing to be severed because of guilt. This condition is not from God, but created by fear. Should we feel this way, though, we are often taught by Christianity to ask forgiveness for our sins, in order to re-connect with God: "*If we confess our sins, he is faithful and just to forgive us our sins and to cleanse us from all unrighteousness*" (I John 1:9 KJV). This approach to spirituality is never freeing, for it makes people feel as though they are a yo-yo on the end of a string. Such a Christian life can become full of emotional ups and downs, coinciding with every success and failure. This is why so many suffer under the doctrines of Christianity and cannot find freedom or peace. These feelings of doubt and guilt are fear, and it is created because we do not understand who we are. Because we choose to perceive ourselves as being separate from God; therefore, we believe we are condemned. Our relationship with Spirit (God), however, cannot be based upon duality. Either the whole of humanity is indeed separated from God for all eternity, or we are truly already one with the Divine and simply remain aware. I choose to see our connection, not separation. Whatever may seem threatened, in this case our relationship with God, cannot be real. It is up to the individual to decide when enough is enough. Would an incorrupt God create people who are corrupt? Do you believe you are born condemned, and in need of rescue from, and by, a wrathful god? Or, would you rather know that you are a dynamic, worthy, loved, divinely-imbued Spirit? The choice is yours. Only you can decide what you allow your mind to believe; otherwise, it will ultimately, and unknowingly, deceive.

It should come to no surprise that if we are part of the eternal Spirit, obviously we have always been. In some form or fashion, in Spirit, all of us have existed. If we are a part of the whole, that is perfect and eternal, then the true me cannot be made corruptible. I, too, must be eternally incorruptible. We are already perfect, whole and have always existed. It is quite possible, that some of us may not remember our former existence right now. But, we have existed. There are some passages I feel are worth mentioning that do indeed point to this:

> "*For those God foreknew he also predestined to be*

*conformed to the likeness of his Son, that he might be the firstborn among many brothers."* - Romans 8:29 (NIV)

I like to share this verse from Paul, as it does reveal a couple things concerning who we are. The Spirit foreknew us, before our earthly existence. Therefore, we existed prior and are all in the divine plan. Even more interesting, this passage shares that Yeshua is not higher in rank (as one might think a solitary god would be) than any of us. He is simply called the firstborn, meaning he was an early example of, and for, many who would come after him. Yeshua was a model, for all of mankind, of those who would know their eternal connection with the divine Spirit.

Psalm 139 also points to our pre-existence and eternal nature:

"For You formed my inward parts; You covered me in my mother's womb. I will praise You, for I am fearfully and wonderfully made; Marvelous are Your works, And that my soul knows very well. My frame was not hidden from You, When I was made in secret, And skillfully wrought in the lowest parts of the earth. Your eyes saw my substance, being yet unformed. And in Your book they all were written, The days fashioned for me, When as yet there were none of them." - Psalm 139:13-16 (NKJV)

David knew that he existed prior to coming into a physical body. The physical body is perhaps created to serve a purpose, and thus has its natural conclusion, as it is a temporary vessel. But, the Spirit is eternal, and thankfully who we really are. Yeshua sought to facilitate spiritual people who would look to the eternal within them. As we explored, the Christian idea that we are separate from the eternal, being destined for spiritual death unless rescued, opposes the message of Yeshua. There is a huge difference between awakening to the truth that we are already eternal Spirit, and the Christian teaching that we must somehow receive eternal life. Why would one need to receive something they already have? To believe we must become eternal is illogical.

Let's examine what Christianity calls the "Holy Spirit" and explore its meaning. The words, translated as *"Holy Spirit"* or *"Holy Ghost"* in both the Greek and Hebrew texts of the Bible, mean "sacred breath." To become aware of the *sacred breath* is to awaken to the eternal Spirit within you. It's finding the real you. Some call this awakening, a step toward enlightenment, or in Christian terminology it could be equated with what Yeshua meant when he spoke of salvation. The more one is awake to the Spirit within, the more the person will listen to the *sacred breath* as a *"knowing within."* The gentle leading of the inward Spirit brings one to remembrance of the truth which was already there, but seemed temporarily forgotten.

Becoming aware of the *sacred breath* is what many
Christians describe as *being filled with the Spirit.* I can
distinctly remember when I first recognized Spirit,
and the voice within me. It was a turning point in my
life. Some within charismatic Christianity might call
this the *"baptism of the Spirit,"* the same as what others
deem as being *"Spirit-filled."* The use of the word
"filled," may imply to people that we can somehow
become empty of Spirit and need more. This, simply,
is not so. The Spirit is part of you and can never be
lost, though we *can* turn away from listening to this
inner guide. When we are sensitive to the Spirit
within, we easily discern the *sacred breath*, the voice of
the eternal as our being. This voice gently leads us
*"unto all truth,"* as Yeshua stated. So, to be filled with
the Spirit is to be aware of, and in-tune with, the true
you.

The *sacred breath* is our connection with others, not
only people in physical bodies, but people on the
other side of the grave. Through the Spirit, ideas,
thoughts and guidance can be received by the careful
listener. It can be like tuning into a far away radio
broadcast with only a hand held receiver. When we
listen closely, messages can be detected and
understood. Yeshua referenced these messages when
he taught about his interaction with his "heavenly
Father." *Heaven* depicts Spirit, the "higher place"

found within each person. In contrast, the earth
symbolizes the lower, bodily part of mankind. We are
aware of our bodies and that we had natural parents -
a physical mother and father who brought forth our
earthly existence. Traces of our ancestors can be
found within our physical, genetic make-up.
Similarly, your Spirit is a portion of the whole,
heavenly Father in you. This Father of spirits, that
gives everything existence, is therefore our connection
to all that truly exists. This is the incorruptible, pure
Spirit - the *sacred breath*.

Often, we remain unaware that each of us have others
with us in Spirit, who are gently working to guide
and assist us. Enlightened spirits communicate
through our connection with Spirit. One might
choose to call these higher spirits "angels," a word
which means *messengers*. Messengers collectively
make up one's personal "heavenly Father." Our *Father*
is not a frightening deity living on a throne up in the
sky, but a caring Spirit who watches over us. And
this one Spirit is made up of many within.

The *heavenly Father*, Yeshua mentioned and followed
during his ministry, was revealed by him to a few of
his disciples according to a passage in the Bible.
Many call this event "the Mount of Transfiguration,"
where we read of Yeshua communicating with Moses
and Elijah in the presence of Peter, James and John:

> "*After six days Jesus took with him Peter, James*

*and John the brother of James, and led them up a high mountain by themselves. There he was transfigured before them. His face shone like the sun, and his clothes became as white as the light. Just then there appeared before them Moses and Elijah, talking with Jesus." - Matthew 17:1-3 (NIV)*

Christians are primarily taught from this passage that Yeshua's appearance changed temporarily. Whether his countenance changed or not, is irrelevant. The real point of the story is that Yeshua, who we read stated that he followed what *his* heavenly Father showed him to do (John 5:19), revealed he was having a two-way communication with spirits on the other side of the grave. This passage suggests that Yeshua's heavenly Father was not a single deity communicating with him, but the all-encompassing Spirit from which Moses, Elijah and probably other enlightened beings spoke. Could this also be why we read in the Gospels that Yeshua cried out for his Father, *Elijah*, when he died on the cross (Matthew 27:46-49), and that *Elijah* spoke through John the Baptist, as well (Matthew 11:14; 17:12)? Elijah, it would seem, was very busy speaking with Yeshua, John the Baptist and quite possibly others during this important time in history. Having a higher perspective from which to share, Elijah and Moses could have provided enlightened guidance to Yeshua through the Spirit. My main point, in sharing such an idea, is that we should learn we never are separate from others, for the Spirit connects us all.

Christianity's teachings of separation, from each other and from God, were never taught by Yeshua, for we can find evidence of this even within the Christian New Testament.

Those, who recognize the Spirit speaking to them, typically ascribe it to being the "voice of God." And, though the Spirit is the Divine speaking within us, we should understand that the same Spirit is within all people. To put it another way, all people are within the same Spirit. We often remain unaware, that when we receive an idea, a thought, a confirmation, or a good word, it can originate from another who is lovingly interacting with our lives in Spirit. We naturally want to believe all our thoughts are our own. Let us consider, for a moment, that we possibly could receive thoughts from someone else unseen. Have you ever had an idea come to you, or a thought about someone or something, that didn't seem to originate from within your own head? I certainly have, and formerly believed that all my thoughts originated from either myself, or God.

When I chaired an elders committee at a Christian church, I would pray for direction, looking for guidance to help us lead the congregation. I had desired to know and do God's will. When I would quiet my mind by mentally detaching from the physical realm through meditation, I would listen for wisdom deep within me. During these times, I would receive answers and insights, often feeling a tangible presence come upon me. In my mind, at the time, I thought, "*This has to be God. Who else could it be?*" Through the years, the more I listened, the more was revealed to me. Over time, I was gently shown that spirits from the other side, who were enlightened, speak with me. What I had initially thought to be a single God outside of me, I now perceive as being many people in Spirit assisting me on my life-journey. Some people call such ministering spirits "angels" or "spirit guides." Similarly, the Bible claims Jesus was assisted by angels, too:

> "*...angels came and ministered to him.*" - Matthew 4:11 (KJV)

If spirit messengers did in fact interact with Yeshua, then why couldn't they attend to our lives also? Could people, who have shed their physical bodies through death, still have concern for those of us here on Earth? I would suggest they do care, much more than we might know. Allow me to share my translation of an interesting verse concerning people, after physical death, becoming like angels:

> "*Upon living again (in the next plane), people will not marry, or be given in marriage. They will be like the angels (messengers) of the divine Spirit.*" - Matthew 22:30

When I first understood angels as being messengers in Spirit, and not mythical, winged-beings with halos,

I wondered, "*Could some people on the other side fill that role in our lives?*" This made perfect sense to me. I knew I was receiving messages from Spirit, and where there is a message, there has to be a messenger. I only had to look to the world around me to realize that all people are messengers. Our messages may vary, but everyone has a voice that affects others. Yeshua touched on this concept when he told Nathaniel that he would see heaven opened (revealed) and "*the angels of God ascending and descending upon the son of man*" (John 1:51 KJV). To me, this statement describes the influence of others, invisibly assisting us for the better. When we look to Yeshua as an example, we read he was not earthly led, but instead guided by the Spirit, his higher place of existence (allow me to equate our higher, elevated being with "heaven"). By explaining the affairs of heaven for us, Yeshua revealed a higher, inward communication does indeed take place with Spirit messengers.

A couple more stumbling blocks need to be removed for some people before their own, inner communication with Spirit can be established. By re-visiting the Gospel of John one more time, the Christian idea of worship can be addressed. Ironically, worshiping God can be another way to disconnect one from their source. Christianity often gives the wrong idea of worship. Let us read a quote from Yeshua, found in the Bible, regarding the Spirit who guides us:

> *"...the true honorer, honors the Father in Spirit and in truth... God is Spirit, and those who honor, must honor in Spirit and truth."* - John 4:23-24

This passage is typically translated using the word "worship" (in place of honor) which incorrectly implies we must bow down, essentially paying our dues to an external, fearful God who has spared us. *To honor*, or *revere*, better conveys the idea that we should hold the Spirit, which is God, up to higher esteem than we hold our outer-shell, the *visible me*. We do so by respecting the Spirit of Truth for our guidance. This is how we honor and revere the Spirit, *in spirit* and in truth. There is no god outside of us. Should we think otherwise, we mentally separate ourselves from the Divine, refusing to receive life-giving guidance from our deepest source. I cannot say this any plainer: the Spirit within you *is* God, *your* heavenly Father. Listen to your Father.

Christians are often fearful of leaving religion behind, laying their Bible down, and casting out into life, trusting only to be guided by Spirit. Scripture verses, Bible classes and even ministers are not needed for the Spirit to guide and teach us. A religion, such as Christianity, is not required to communicate with God. Lessons for life can be found anywhere, and the Spirit will choose what tools are necessary to best reveal truth to the individual. A simple walk in the woods has at times been a place where the inner guide has spoken to me through use of nature. Other times, my children have been used to wake me up to truths. For example, I can distinctly recall my younger son sharing a dream with me when he was about eight years old. It was interesting to watch him attempt to convey what he had learned about another plane of existence, what I deem as being the Spirit realm. In his dream, he was shown that we interact within multiple realms simultaneously, because we are truly spirits having both a physical and spiritual experience. This revelation was huge for such a young man, and it was not a concept I had previously shared with him. At the time, it seemed coincidental that I had formerly received the same revelation through the Spirit within me, but now I realize my son's dream is an awesome confirmation to the voice inside my being.

Our minds seem to continually race with thoughts of daily events, upcoming tasks, ideas, hopes, worries, and other emotions. To be able to connect with our source, which is Spirit, we must first learn to quiet the thoughts within our heads. In order to do that, it is impossible to look outside of ourselves and still hear the truth that waits within. The sights and sounds of the world around us is unknowingly our distraction, appealing to our five senses, and so often, alluring. Yet, deep inside of us, there remains a small, still voice, begging to be heard over all the clamor. It is ever pointing, ever striving to lead us unto all truth. The Spirit is where the journey begins and nowhere else.  The door is before you already; you needn't go anywhere.  Simply, open the door by quieting your mind and listening.  What do you hear within you?

Following the lead of the higher being is essential to finding direction for one's life.  To choose to silence such wisdom could be equated to flying an airplane without navigational equipment.  Do you want to soar through life without direction?  If you choose to forsake the guiding Spirit, where do you expect to go, and in what condition will you be in when you arrive?  Is it possible our priorities are, at times, out of order?  People in Yeshua's time also had concerns with physical requirements.  And, in no way am I implying that we should ignore the needs of our physical existence.  I am, however, suggesting that perhaps we can first turn to higher wisdom found within us.  Allow that to be our guide through life:

> *"But seek first the reign of Spirit and its character, and one's true needs will be met."* - Matthew 6:33

Know your never-ending connection with the Divine.  Spirit is not only the source of love, truth, peace, and joy, but is the righteous, pure you.  By seeking that which is real, the rest will come into place, as one's life path is discovered and love is experienced to the fullest.  Our lives are personal journeys unto knowledge.  Today, will you listen for the voice of the Spirit that resides within?  For when we do, light will begin to shine forth, illuminating the road before us.

Fear will be dispelled, and love will be our reward.

# Sources, References & Recommended Reading

## Bibles:

*Holy Bible, New International Version*®, *NIV*®, Copyright© 1973, 1978, 1984 by International Bible Society and Zondervan Corporation LLC.

*New King James Version*®, Copyright © 1982 by Thomas Nelson, Inc.

*Holy Bible, New Living Translation*, Copyright 1996, 2004. Tyndale House Publishers, Inc., Wheaton, Illinois 60189.

*New American Standard Bible*®, Copyright © 1960, 1962, 1963, 1968, 1971, 1972, 1973, 1975, 1977, 1995 by The Lockman Foundation.

*Interlinear Greek-English New Testament*, © 1981 George Ricker Berry, Baker Book House Company.

*The Holy Bible*, 1611 Authorized King James Version by the Church of England.

## Bible Reference Books:

*Strong's Exhaustive Concordance of the Bible*, James Strong, S.T.D., LL.D, Hendrickson Publishers, Peabody Massachusetts.

*Vine's Expository Dictionary of New Testament Words*, Hendrickson Publishers, Peabody Massachusetts.

## Books:

*Misquoting Jesus: The Story Behind Who Changed the Bible and Why*, © 2005 Bart D. Ehrman, Harper One Publishers.

*The Lost Religion of Jesus: Simple Living and Non-Violence in Early Christianity*, © 2001 Keith Akers, Lantern Books.

*Harper's Dictionary of Classical Antiquities*, 1897 Harry Thurston Peck, Prof. of Columbia University, Harpers & Brothers Publishers.

*The Origin and History of the Doctrine of Endless Punishment*, 1855, Thomas B. Thayer, University Publishing House.

*The Summa Theologica of St. Thomas Aquinas, Second and Revised Edition*, 1920, Fathers of the English Dominican Province.

*The City of God, Volume II*, by St. Augustine, translated by Marcus Dods, 1871,T. & T. Clark.

*The Encyclopedia of Angels, Second Edition*, © 2004 Rosemary Ellen Guiley, Checkmark Books.

*The Encyclopedia of Ghosts and Spirits, Second Edition*, © 2000 Rosemary Ellen Guiley, Checkmark Books.

## On-line Resources:
*The Milton Reading Room*, Luxon, Thomas H., ed., http://www.dartmouth.edu/~milton, October, 2008.

*Internet Medieval Sourcebook*, Fordham University Center for Medieval Studies, http://www.fordham.edu/halsall/sbook.html, 2006.

*Early Church Texts*, Reverend Andrew Maguire, MA, BD, http://www.earlychurchtexts.com, 2003.

*The Original Catholic Encyclopedia*, 1914, http://oce.catholic.com, San Diego Catholic Answers 2007.

*The Catholic Encyclopedia*, 1917 New Advent, http://www.newadvent.org/cathen/.

*The Gnosis Archive*, Lance Owens, http://www.gnosis.org, 1995-2009.

*Early Christian Writings*, Peter Kirby, http://www.earlychristianwritings.com, 2001-2006.

*International World History Project*, World History Project USA, http://world-history.org, 2007.

*Livius: Articles on Ancient History*, Jona Lendering, http://www.livius.org, 2008.

*Gateways to Babylon*, Lishtar, http://www.gatewaystobabylon.com, 2000.

*Tentmaker*, Gary and Michell Amirault, http://www.tentmaker.org, Tentmaker Ministeries, 2008.

*On Doctrine*, Gary Hand, http://www.ondoctrine.com, 2002.

*Encyclopædia Brittanica*, Encyclopædia Britannica, Inc., http://www.brittanica.com, 2008.

*MSN Encarta Encyclopedia*, http://encarta.msn.com, 2008.

*Merriam-Webster On-line Dictionary*, http://www.merriam-webster.com, Merriam Webster Inc, 2008.

*BibleGateway.com*, http://www.biblegateway.com, Zondervan Corporation LLC, 2008.

*Dybbuk - Spirit Possession and Jewish Folklore*, Jeff Balanger, http://www.ghostvillage.com, Ghost Village, November 29, 2003.

*Wikipedia*, Wikimedia Foundation, Inc., http://wikipedia.org, 2008.

*Association of Unity Churches,* http://www.unity.org, 2008.

*Unitarian Universalist Association of Churches,* http://www.uua.org, 2008.

*The Church of Christ, Scientist,* http://www.tfccs.com, 2008.

Made in the USA